LEFT BEHIND

LEFT BEHIND

Journeys into British Politics

David Selbourne

JONATHAN CAPE
THIRTY-TWO BEDFORD SQUARE
LONDON

First published 1987
Copyright © 1987 by David Selbourne

Jonathan Cape Ltd, 32 Bedford Square, London WC1B 3EL

British Library Cataloguing in Publication Data

Selbourne, David
Left behind.
I. Socialism —— Great Britain
I. Title
335'.00941   HX244
ISBN 0 224 02370 5

Phototypeset by Falcon Graphic Art Ltd
Wallington, Surrey
Printed and bound in Great Britain by
The Camelot Press Ltd, Southampton

FOR DONALD AND CAROL

Contents

For my part I am quite willing that any reader should say sometimes that I have not observed correctly, provided that he himself will observe better.

La Bruyère

Introduction

This is the record of a personal struggle, as well as of a gradually losing economic, social and cultural battle in Britain; a struggle to square my own long-standing ('left') sentiment and conviction with the inconvenient truths of things observed in my journeys for *New Society*. These journeys took me to superficially dreary or 'ordinary' places, where I found – as well as older hopes and expectations, and familiar forms of contention – an underworld, often unemployed, of new anxieties and suspicions. I encountered not only brave plans and programmes to 'deal with the crisis', but complicated tensions and hatreds too; disconcerting signs and portents, as decent (and sometimes indecent) people wrestled with, and over, the consequences of our economic contraction, industrial decline, inner-city decay and educational failure. The wounds of Britain, those of a profound disordering and dislocation, are deep, and bleeding; and not least because, as never before, what are dreams to some are nightmares to others, often their next-door neighbours.

It is a more complex and 'transitional' picture which emerges, the closer the unsentimental attention paid with eye and ear to its faces and voices, gestures, words and bodies. Again inconveniently for 'left' and 'right' alike, it presents us with currents of feeling, political 'positions' and moral judgments which make nonsense of every interpretative schema, most prejudices, and all our glib assumptions as to what the Tom, Dick and Harry of fable think – or ought to think, if only they knew better – about their own or others' condition. Thus, the real Tom, Dick and Harry (or Jill, Jane and Judy), actually attended to, allowed to speak, and respected as individuals – rather than as abstract members of a class, or mass, in some political-geometrical theorem – step immediately out of that cardboard world which the all-knowing ideologue himself inhabits.

Oh, they have served us ill, so many of our respected 'left' and 'socialist' teachers in particular, alchemists, magicians and pedlars of half-truth – I say nothing here of rank Lysenko-like untruth – in the guise of academic or scientific rigour; have themselves disordered our understandings and clouded our perceptions even of what lies under our noses and at our very elbows, with their sentimental fictions; the greatest those which concern the nature and culture, politics and prospects of the working class. Giant Falsehood, straining at a gnat, or a place in the sun of 'socialist' estimation, has not merely shouted down *vox populi*, but has erected sandbagged barricades of further falsification and erudition against those who would discover, or rediscover, the 'left's' long history of intellectual failure. Yet 'left' salesmen of so many exhausted explanatory concepts, remote from (and therefore incapable of explaining) the quotidian round, continue to call their wares, or frayed stock-in-trade, in ways which have become no more than formulaic incantations.

Is this not a paradox? After all, 'socialism', as a philosophy and practice of the 'social' – 'social-ism' – can mean, and has meant, whatever politicians, philosophers and activists have wished it to mean. Its early nineteenth-century origin as a word and as a concept is clear enough, however; it was a morality which distinguished itself from that which gave priority to the 'individual'. And in the light of this morality, the 'social question' – the condition of the people – was seen as demanding remedial social action. But the counterposing of the 'social' and the 'individual' in this way was, *ab initio*, artificial, uneasy, schematic; and itself did not, and never will, correspond to the real world of real (that is, individual-*and*-social) human beings. In this world, the two terms can have no objective existence as separable categories, as entities in themselves, nor serve as guides to distinct forms of political action.

Today, the word 'socialism' is more ambiguous, put to more tormented uses, and is less significant than ever. Indeed, within the largest and most powerful industrial capitalist society in the world, the USA, it is not even a marginal domestic issue. Moreover, it makes not the slightest practical difference whether one regards the British Labour Party, for example, as 'socialist' or not; the definition of the word and the criteria for its absence or presence in practice are so unstable and so dependent upon the eye of the beholder that neither the point nor the counterpoint is any longer worth making. Worse still, in Britain there are at least two very different 'socialist traditions' – broadly speaking, statist and centralist on the one hand, anti-statist or voluntarist on the other – and each of them as capable of being given a 'right-wing' as a 'left-wing' connotation. In such circumstances, the debate about whether the Labour Party is, was, or ought to be 'socialist' becomes more than ever a game of intellectual blindman's buff; or a parlour game of *a priori* assertion and *ex post facto* rationalization.

Some things, however, are plain enough. First, 'socialism's' ends (however defined, however pursued) must be bound to the interests of the real human being, whether perceived in his/her social context or 'outside' it. 'Socialism', to justify itself at all, must prosper this real human being (a 'subject' of 'flesh and blood'); it is not sufficient to satisfy mere abstractions, whether of 'class' and 'mass' or of the planners' computer programs. Second, the 'right' has in the last years mounted an increasingly disruptive challenge to the 'left's' sense of what the interests of this 'individual' are. But the 'left's' dilemma, whatever its electoral fortunes, is that though it *must* reclaim this ground from the 'right' – and is now seeming to do so – it *cannot*. Why not? Because of the taboo, or fetish, which persistently elevates the abstractly 'social' or 'collective' over the claims of the 'individual', and crudely equates concern with, and interest in, the latter with the instinct of the 'bourgeois' or 'petit-bourgeois'. Hence, thirdly, it is not surprising that citizen rights (civic rights, human rights, the Rights of Man, precisely as defined in 1789) against the State, against tyranny, against arbitrariness, against bureaucracy, against monopoly, against exploitation and the threat of annihilation, remain in the custody of, and have come to be defended by, some of 'socialism's' bitterest opponents.

Equally plain is that 'we have eyes and ears', as Goethe told Eckermann, 'only for what we know'. So it is that in Britain, now as ever, one socialist envisages, for a fee, a 'new' left tactics of alliance; a second, competing for attention, proposes as a 'way forward' – to what? – the setting up of yet another 'new' left party; a third detects in plebeian reaction itself, fighting for its market bargains, a revival of an old proletarian spirit; a fourth sagely magicks away inconvenient and unassimilable truths, transmuting them – by intellectual sleight of hand – into 'contradictions'; a fifth, bent over his desk, raises his nose to the wind and sniffs (for *Marxism Today*, or the *Guardian*) a renaissance of 'left' fortunes or the renewed onset of 'class struggle'; a sixth pays a mortgage or school-fees with slabs of left rhetoric in the ('unfree') liberal media. Together, they refuse to be disturbed in their own shibboleths as to what constitutes a true progress; and no wonder, when for any doctrine of 'socialism' now to recover its sense of direction is such a tall order. Why? Because a radically and genuinely revised conception of the 'social', and therefore of 'social-ism', must be predicated on Britain's industrial contraction, on the cross-class acceptance of the market and property system, and on the centrality of our culture's regard for the rights of the 'individual', as well as on the irreversible rejection of existing 'socialist' models of state and economic organization.

None of these problems is fortuitous. For behind the general intellectual failure of this socialist generation, to go back no further, stand many factors, and many levels at which they must be considered: failures of method, errors helplessly committed by a privileged (alternative ruling-class) 'Marxism', failures induced by simplistic or puritan views of the meanings of nineteenth-century working-class struggles; and failures of understanding – with rare exceptions – both of the complex impact of the Industrial Revolution on working people, and of their inconvenient aspirations. But at the deepest epistemological level, where a century and more of 'left' corpses moulder, is the paradox that the observation of events themselves, and the capacity to respond to what Marx called 'real, sensory actuality' – the actuality of the human individual – have come to be blocked, not crowned, by 'Marxism'.

How? Because just as a stagecoach may be turned back into a pumpkin, so 'Marxism', for most of its intellectually-dependent and easily-scared practitioners, has been reduced to a set of invariant principles as to the primacy of this or that form of social order, and this or that cluster of actors and activities in the division of labour. The consequences for the 'left's' tormented intellectual performance – which has created what Vico called *'un mondo di forme'* – have been fatal; disabling understanding not only of the unfamiliar, the new and the unwelcome, but of the particular and the individual also – of all that which, one way or another, does not 'adequately' fit the inherited matrix, set in mental concrete, and the entrenched schema. These are veritably albatrosses hanging around the neck of the free-thinker. As Dickens wrote in *Hard Times*, it is 'as if an astronomical observatory should be made without any windows, and the astronomer within should arrange the starry universe solely by pen, ink and paper'; as if Gradgrind had 'no need to cast an eye upon the teeming myriads of human beings around him, but could settle all their destinies on a slate and wipe out all their tears with one dirty little bit of sponge' – in our times, the sponge of this or that version of 'socialism', welfarism among them.

Indeed, a disencumbered 'left' rereading of the industrializing nineteenth century and of its less comfortable literatures, political and poetic, is urgent if light is to be shed upon the dark myths of the imaginary 'long revolution', say, and upon its fictitious world of 'deepening consciousness', 'progress' and 'contradiction'. There is much at stake, since expectations founded upon such notions have been deeply destructive of our sense of direction, and of a just appraisal of possibility and impossibility in our culture. Instead, what we need to acknowledge, and celebrate, is that the sensibilities of its sharpest

observers are those which are the most discrete and the most
complex, whatever their class origin or political affiliation;
and they insist that we recognize how repetitiously we have
circled the same stones of dull certitude, or leapt from the
same cliff of illusion. (And this despite the seeming-agility of
each generation's 'new left' tumblers.)

To take one example only: open Gustave Flaubert's *Sentimental Education*, completed in 1869. There you will find
him, only twenty years after the publication of the *Communist
Manifesto*, presciently condemning St-Simon, Fourier and
Cabet as men who, their 'socialism' notwithstanding, themselves 'wanted to reduce mankind ... . and tie it to the bench
and counter'; precisely as the politics of the 'proletariat', both
in theory and practice, was to reduce it. Or you will find him
describing his 'radical' republican intellectual Sénécal – and
Flaubert's were characters taken closely from life – as a 'man of
theory' who 'respected only the masses [but] was merciless
towards individuals'. Flaubert even presents us, in early form,
with that archetype of our culture, 'the gentleman . . .
affecting a humble manner, talking the language of the plebs,
and leaving his hands unwashed to make them look horny. To
obtain a reputation for common sense', Flaubert added (nearly
120 years ago!), 'it was necessary to use the following expression as often as possible: . . . "social problem" and "workshop".' Is all this comic, or tragic?

The fact that history, 'working-class history' in particular,
teaches us more ambiguous lessons than most of the 'left' (like
the 'right') is willing to recognize and assimilate is not a matter
of 'ignorance', plain or simple. Instead, it is a suppressed
knowledge, known by 'socialists' only to be forgotten, or to be
subjected to a rhetorical reduction. But it is in such displacements and elisions that there resides a large part of the secret
of 'socialism's' ideological failures. How comfortable it is to
forget, but how necessary to remember – to take an example at
random – the declaration of the Chartist leader, Joseph
Stephens, before an audience of 200,000 at the height of the
agitation, that Chartism was 'a knife-and-fork question', and

that the Charter 'means a good house, good food and drink,
prosperity and shorter working hours'; or that Francis Place
sought the repeal of the Combination Acts 'so that men and
masters might be left to themselves . . . to make the best terms
that they could'; or that *before Marx* already-sceptical French
'socialists', Victor Considérant for instance, held that 'the
dream of the definitive and permanent triumph of a party is
. . . an absurdity. It is to suppose', he wrote in 1836, 'that one
social interest could succeed in extinguishing all the others,
which fortunately is impossible.' And that was twelve years
before the *Manifesto*. 'Today,' wrote Constantin Pecqueur in
1846, 'people [sc. 'socialists'] place their hopes in solidarity
and the tacit or actual association of workers. They believe in a
permanent, fully conscious league of labour against capital, of
wages against profit . . . One fears it to be an illusory outlook.'
The fear was justified.

Indeed now, just as then, what 'really goes on' in the
'grass-roots' (a term which is itself both ugly and alienated)
often fails to correspond sufficiently, or at all, to the figments
of the 'left' ideological imagination; inadequately grounded in
experience as it is, and whose distinction between 'theory' and
'practice' is a distinction between two disjoined spheres of
endeavour. (Some of those who know this have gone to the
other extreme, and are now in turn – and in their 'workshops'
– unable to see the wood for the trees.) 'You are misled',
Alexander Herzen warned his already-deaf nineteenth-century
'socialist' contemporaries, 'by categories not fitted to catch the
flow of life . . . You can be as angry as you like, but you will
not change the world to fit a programme. It goes its own way
. . . Life is infinitely more stubborn than theory.'

This book's reports of four years of intermittent journeys,
up-hill and down-dale, turned out to be – they were certainly
not intended as such – a record of this 'stubbornness'. In each
case, but diminishing as time passed, I set out with my own
stock-in-trade of emotionally and intellectually 'orthodox'
expectation; to return abashed by how threadbare and ex-
perientially bogus were the assumptions and the hopes, the

words and the reflexes, which normally signify and express such expectations; confused as to, and struggling to decipher, the meanings which might be given to what I was seeing and hearing. Eventually, I was to set all this down in theoretical terms in my book *Against Socialist Illusion: A Radical Argument*, published early in 1985. But what went into the making and remaking of my belief in the urgent necessity for a thoroughly heretical and dissident literature of the 'left', a genuinely radical literature, were – together with my twenty years at Ruskin – the complex and awkward encounters which follow: steps on the long road to a greater intellectual freedom.

At the time I made copious notes, *verbatim*, of what was said to me; and each place, however mean and unpromising a terrain at first sight, became a world of argument as discourse unfolded, and as 'the culture' took on its often embarrassing depths of meaning. Such habits of attention and record that I may have brought with me to the task were usefully learned in more (or equally?) unfamiliar places, in India for example, on which I have written both in retrospection and in the heat of the journalistic moment. In my notes, I sought throughout to do detailed justice to the density and intricacy of comment, appearance and context; and always included gesture and intonation, nuance and silence, as 'facts', or at least as grist to the mill of perception.

There may be, indeed there is, artifice as well as artfulness in what follows; the structuralist and semiotician would insist upon it. But then one man's meat was always another's poison, and not only in Bradford; the deepest social or cultural truth to some is the most arrant and tendentious of falsehoods to others. More troubling to me was that under constraints of time and space, worried by deadlines and the risk of the editor's scissors, I gave too short shrift in the original truncated versions of these pieces to what I had seen and heard. Each chapter of this book is therefore now what I had intended, ideally, at the time; expanded – very substantially so in some cases and places – but not rewritten. That is, I have returned to my notebooks, avoided hindsight and the retailoring of impression and judgment, whether those of witnesses or my own; and, free of constraint, added, filled out and restored what had originally to be excluded. The excuse for the fuller re-presentation, in chronological order of writing, of this evidence of our growing unease is that even if the individuals involved fade from the scene, the issues that between them they raise will not, because they cannot. (In the Afterword, I have added a brief note on the later circumstances of some of the protagonists in these pages.)

I am grateful to past students at Ruskin, including Eddie Bannon, John Clifford, Joy Copley, John Healy, Rob Humphreys, Dave McMonnies, Tom Mole, Tony Stewart and Hyacinth Wilson, who helped me to find my way in the communities they came from; to Graham Greene of Jonathan Cape for his encouragement of my work; and, of course, to Paul Barker, former editor of *New Society*, for four years of stimulus, support and collaboration. In *Sentimental Education*, Deslauriers, the out-at-elbows lawyer, is for ever daydreaming of 'an editor's chair, in other words, the ineffable joy of controlling other people, of carving up their articles, of commissioning copy and of then turning it down'. No Deslauriers he, Paul Barker was instead the 'hidden hand' behind the sustaining of a substantial amount of the effort, including my own, in documentary writing on today's Britain; and much else besides. Indeed, his tenure of the paper's editorship from 1968 to 1986 made *New Society* into one of the most open and innovative of journals; hospitable to the widest forms of cultural and social inquiry, free of cant and with a range of debate not found in the closed and collusive worlds of politically more partisan writing.

I must also thank Sybil Brooke once again for her typing; and, above all, my wife, who is the co-author of my better judgments. Any misjudgments are my own.

Elsfield, Oxford D.S.

Phlegm, in the Pennine Foothills

December 1981

'Is it an emergency? What's wrong, love?' 'What name is it, pet?' 'What's he done, love?'

The phones don't stop ringing. It is 8.30 a.m. Behind them, the medical records – 17,000 of them, or half the population's – stand on metal racks. It is all women's voices, white coats, Dr Scholl's wooden sandals, broad vowels and the first brew-up of the morning.

This is Hyde, in Tameside, on the Lancashire-Cheshire border, land of Lowry (and Myra Hindley), made – and unmade – by cotton. If the Pennines can be said to have foothills, then we are in them. When the light came up, with a sharp October nip in the air, it was not so much rosy-fingered as the colour of liver sausage; you could see your breath in it. (Round here, the word 'love' sometimes seems the only beacon in the darkness.) I am in the Clarendon House group practice, beside the bus station, as the morning rush hour of the halt, the lame and the anxious begins to press in on its seven doctors.

A fat chap with a moustache, hair down his shoulders, and with a beery paunch hanging over his trousers, appears at the reception window. 'What time do you want, love?' 'I'm not bothered.' 'Your address, please, love.' He gives it. 'Half-past eight on Friday morning. Will that do, love?' 'Ta.' A man on crutches, in blue denim and with tattooed fingers, limps down the yellow linoleum. 'They're at the window,' Dr David Livingstone, the head of the practice, said to me later, speaking of the six ladies at the counter, 'they see a lot.' But he sees more; opening your shirt or blouse, or dropping your pants, is more than merely coming out from behind northern lace-curtains.

This is a dismal neck of the woods, if ever there was one, with 3,000 jobless in the town, with chronically low wages – 10 per cent below the national average in textiles, 20 per cent below in clothing and footwear – and with the staple industries declining; with above-average infant mortality, black plastic bags for the rubbish, and the town-centre cinemas turned to bingo. 'There is a pervading atmosphere of physical neglect throughout Tameside,' says an official profile of the area, but 'no obvious growth sector in the local economy has been discovered'. Martin Webster has marched here, too – 'a provocation', Dr Livingstone called it – protected by the police in hundreds, and at a cost of tens of thousands.

Unemployment, says Alan Bruce, the 'senior research officer' at the town hall, 'rose very quickly after the Conservative government came in, when you got the big closures at Tootal's and Courtauld's. We used to say to ourselves, "We may not be prosperous, but at least we're stable." Four or five years ago, there used to be a lot of optimism round here, but it's all gone now. The problem is not just unemployment, but the bottom dropping out of the local economy.' There is 15·8 per cent unemployment in the Tameside area, an increase of 186 per cent between 1979 and 1981; the national increase was 103 per cent in the same period. And in Lancashire, in the third quarter of 1981 alone, there have been 366 bankruptcies and liquidations. There is no 'bottoming out' of the recession here; no 'upturn'.

The prospect, says the local report, is 'disturbing'. But if the economists weigh the statistics of it, and the politicians bemoan it, it is the doctor who has to treat it – as services falter, waiting-lists lengthen and shadows deepen. Yet here, in the large waiting-room, clean as a clinic and shining with polish, faces seem impassive. 'Be a patient patient,' it says on the wall. They are, or seem to be. Browsing through the *North Cheshire Herald and Hyde Reporter*, I see that Stalybridge Celtic have been 'humiliated', four-nil, by Prescot Cables. 'It was pathetic fare,' writes their man at the match, 'with nary a semblance of challenge, spirit or resistance. For this current Celtic side, defeat simply does not hurt enough.' Perhaps that explains it. 'Tebbit takes on the unions,' screams the *Sun*. No one bats an eyelid. Drs Beenstock, Bennett, Farrar, Livingstone and McGillivray await them. The colour supplements, together with *Cosmopolitan* and *Woman*, stand in neat piles on the table. It is all running like clockwork.

Hyde is not quite the place I remember from my own wartime childhood in the area. In those days, it was – or seems to be in memory – all bruise-coloured brick, looming crowded mills, and rookeries of crouching terraces and dark ginnels; a place of smoking chimneys, sooty privet and blackened churches. My father was a doctor in neighbouring Dukinfield, three miles away; and, through him, I see it still as a world of asthma, bandy-legs and bronchitis. In our wartime waiting-room – dingy and coal-lit, and smelling of the sourness of defeat and poor bodies – the patients used to sit in a muffled fug of coughing and spitting, reading *Picture Post*, *Blighty* and *Reveille* till the pages fell apart in grey, dog-eared tatters. Today's anti-rickets posters are in Urdu.

In a starched white coat – 'in them days' – my father spent his life on these towns' bodies, which always seemed to be sick and tired. It was as if everybody was bowed down, bent double, by labour. In the wind, before the Clean Air Act, the whorls of smut and smoke would swirl and billow in the down-draughts, roof-pots rattling. The four old cotton towns of Hyde, Stalybridge, Dukinfield and Ashton have always seemed to the people here a world of their own, or what the town hall now calls a 'geographical unit'. In one direction, Salford is far enough away to be foreign; Glossop, in another, is somewhere mountainous, or over the rainbow; while Manchester is the metropolis for a day-out shopping, with the aquarium windows of the buses to Piccadilly always – in memory – fogged and running with condensation. There were 100 cotton mills on the local River Tame as early as 1790: coal-burning and steam-driven, belching and smoking their way through the nineteenth century and into this one, in a district of muck, brass and manufacture, suffocated and always wheezing.

Now, slum clearance has smashed through the terraces, which used to follow each other up-hill and down-dale – in rain, their blue-grey slates like armadillo-plating – leaving more vacancies, and worse dereliction, than the bombs of war. They say 4 per cent of the land in the area is derelict. From here, a bird's eye view would make it 40 per cent. But under this morning's waiting-room neon, and in such polished conditions, the wounds of unemployment and the new depression seem bloodless and centrally heated. Yet this single-storey utility style of Welfare Britain is also the new working-class wasteland: of communities brought down by clearance, planners and already clapped-out post-war public building.

They built the new Jerusalems round here – and every-where – with warped hardboard and breeze-blocks. It is the wattle-and-daub of the twentieth century, a new desert for an old dunghill; made of show-houses and flyovers and motorway-blue road signs at one end of the spectrum, and, at the other, of the fear and unease of trying to make ends meet as the tide of local unemployment rises.

'They're not coming in such large numbers for "a week on the sick" with a bad back, like they used to,' says Dr Stephen Farrar, one of the partners. 'The chap who has a few weeks off every year I don't see so often. They're frightened', he says, 'of losing their jobs. They fear that firms will look at the sick-list and say, "Who's first?" But they don't cut their throats; at least [laughing] they're not doing it in numbers.'

He has recently seen a personnel manager with 'anxiety-type symptoms'. 'This man has been handling the firm's sackings. It is making him ill,' declares Farrar, 'or, rather, he felt it was making him ill. He doesn't like doing it. It isn't very nice for him having to tell people they're out. There is also a continual rumour about ICI,' Farrar adds. (With Walls and Senior Service, they are major local employers.) 'Members of the workforce are jittery there,' he says; among other things, scared of what some local doctors call 'the spiral', which can carry them down from joblessness to unemployability, and a deep drowning. 'But most patients don't talk about it. You have to extract it from them.'

Dr Trewinnard, a young trainee assistant, two months in the practice and himself only twenty-six, has just had a sixteen-year-old girl in who 'doesn't want to do her O levels'; her parents had brought her to the surgery because 'they said she was depressed'. 'I won't get a job anyway,' she had told Trewinnard. 'It was difficult to advise her,' he says, 'because she was justified in being depressed.' What was she depressed about? 'The worth of what she was doing.' Her mother, Trewinnard tells me, thought her daughter had 'an idealistic view of the world. I thought the opposite. She was realistic. But I didn't get anywhere until her mother went out, and I could speak to her on my own. Then she told me that "the good times" were when she was "smashed out of her brain". She wasn't bothered about telling me. It turns out that she is messing about with barbiturates, amphetamines, anything that will "give her a lift". Her mother wanted her to see a psychiatrist; she said her daughter was "disturbed". But I don't think it would help. To me the girl said that she didn't "see any future"; but she wasn't distraught about it.'

Certainly, the well-wrapped waiting-room silence is not what it seems; anxieties are deep-coursing. 'It is a class thing,' says Farrar. 'People of my class think that if they're unemployed, they deserve it. But working-class people are very worried.' 'Brotherhood Is The World's Need' reads a faded nineteenth-century social club signboard on a derelict town-centre building, its windows broken; Gregory Foulds – 'For Quality Furniture' – announces a 'Closing Down Sale: Everything Must Go', in black lettering on a lurid orange ground; while Jean and Ken at the nearby White Lion have a NUPE calendar and a picture of Charles and Diana next to each other on the counter.

In the waiting-room there is a blur of medical posters: 'Anna Ford says, "I would like to help someone live after my death." ' Her lips are pouting, her lipstick glossy; 'Get a donor card from your doctor,' she orders. Her eyes seem to be beckoning and winking. But the come-hither falls flat on these customers, silently waiting for the buzzer and a recipe for their own survival, not someone else's.

Dr Norman Beenstock's position is different. (Or, as Dr Farrar wrily puts it, 'Medical attitudes to the problem of unemployment depend upon your political views, as well as your clinical judgment.') He says: 'The economic climate, the fear of redundancy, is having an effect on people's health. There's more anxiety expressed in hypochondriacal illness, seeking help for minor day-to-day complaints, and depression.' But, according to Beenstock, 'there's a difference of response to recession between the self-employed, the managerial types' – 'those men enjoy their jobs and have a lot to lose, people with some intellectual calibre and a moral conscience' – and what he calls 'the labourers', who are 'still having a long time off for minor aches and pains'; 'still using the system'. ('I find it galling', he says, 'that people are perfectly well on Tuesday, but don't go back to work till the following Monday. But I suppose doctors would do the same', he adds, 'if they had to heave around other people's refuse.') According to him, depressive symptoms are 'commoner higher up the employment ladder'. Livingstone disagrees. 'Unemployment makes the genuine people very depressed, whatever their jobs. It depends on how sensitive you are. But when everybody is suffering – like in the war – people can put up with it better, they can accept it.' Depressed or not, 'the poorer', in Beenstock's terms, 'are still smoking as much as ever' – 'they'll cut down on meat, but not cigarettes' – 'with their colour TVs on from 9 a.m. onwards'.

Out in the town, Lowry's stick-figures have long ago vanished. The tripe shops sell televisions, and Ladbroke's – with Irene, the florist's – rubs shoulders with the Dacca Oriental Delicatessen. The dull uniform of wartime hardship, and the threadbare, patched and grey clothing of northern labour have gone for a Burton. (And so has Burton's.) There are no more knotted kerchiefs and balaclavas, waistcoats without jackets, or shirts without collars; no more clogs and

Bisto-kid faces, no more thin black pumps for children with bony knees and running noses. The view to the Pennines is as clean as a whistle, the grey-green hills delicately snaked and squared with black stone-walling.

'But', says Farrar, 'I'm often in really poor homes. You can't compare the present situation with the 1930s, but some of the houses I go into are filthy.' Filthy? 'There are two groups of poor people here: those who will do everything they can to disguise it, and those who have come to accept it, and just live in dirty conditions. They are a minority; they can't be bothered, and get used to living without carpets. They don't seem to think anything of it, or give the appearance of not caring' – 'this is where the prejudice comes in,' he adds quickly – 'unless the stuff is actually dripping down the walls. They'll have bad chests, and the kids will have recurrent infections. It becomes very difficult to help them. They may take the medicines you prescribe, if you give it them straight; but there is real resistance on an unconscious level' ('it's not wilful') 'to social advice and social workers. It derives from social attitudes in general' – 'most people don't want to talk to social workers about personal matters' – 'not from the awkwardness of the individual. In general, people here usually won't accept that their "medical" problem is actually a row with the wife or neighbours, or unemployment.'

'The smell of poverty has gone,' asserts Farrar. Yet the community is up against it, in a deep depression both medical and economic; the landscape less soiled, but as sallow and downcast as ever. This is a world with a bleak horizon. Half the factories in use were built before 1914, and the population is growing older also. 'The old people seem to live for ever; we used to expect them to die at sixty-five or seventy but now they go on to eighty or ninety,' a doctor at another practice told me, off the record. Old people at home are 'iller than they used to be', but with facilities for them declining; 'the hospitals are full, old people's homes are full, geriatric beds are limited, and the waiting-lists are getting longer,' says Farrar. The level of knowledge among the elderly about diet, declare the doctors, is as low as ever; 'they eat the cheap, filling things, bread instead of meat, and tinned foods'; they 'can't get down to the shops', or 'don't want the bother of cooking'. In consequence, iron deficiency diseases in the aged are still common.

Dr Beenstock is worried, as well as angry, about the run-down in resources – 'right across the board' – though his argument is complex. On the one hand, he has a real fear of a 'breakdown on the clinical front', when 'patients will actually die because of the run-down. Sooner or later something will hit the headlines and people will say, "How disgusting. It shouldn't happen." ' What he calls the 'good disciplinary effects' of welfare cuts are 'overshadowed by the ill-effects of the run-down in the service'. It also 'reduces our job satisfaction' – a 'tremendous frustration,' he calls it – 'because we can no longer provide all that's needed in day-to-day treatment of the people'. On the other hand, 'I am the one who has to say "this or that is not available". I'm getting the anger. People who have had services expect them. It leads to great pressure on us, because as far as the public is concerned, the welfare state is an open-ended system. They make their demands as of right.' ('The degree of dissatisfaction', Farrar had said hopefully, 'is an indication that we are expected to do better. That's good for society, isn't it?') 'And since the doctor, for many people, is their main contact with the welfare system, it is the doctor who gets the bashing for its defects. If it doesn't tally with their expectations, we get their phlegm.' Phlegm? 'Yes, phlegm.' It is a good bronchitic metaphor, drawn from practice.

'All my work', says Haskell Isaacs, in lightly-accented English – he came to Ashton-under-Lyne from Baghdad in 1948 – 'has been among the British working class; I intended to go to America, but I met my wife here, and she didn't want to.' An ex-Iraqi Army doctor installed in Ashton's dingy Trafalgar Square – 'I spent most of my time in Iraq going around on mule or horseback, in Kurdistan mainly' – he has an MD from Baghdad, and a Lancashire Irish receptionist in red slippers. ' "*Salaam aleikum*," I say in Arabic to my Pakistani patients. They like it very much,' he adds, laughing. Outside is the blackened redbrick of Ashton's late-Victorian Gothic – 'a depressed area, pulled down,' he calls it – set in a tumbled desert of demolition. Inside, on the waiting-room wall, hangs a coloured reproduction of Mecca's 'Holy Ka'Aba at Dusk', painted by 'Azmet Sheikh, of 43/A2, Gulbarg 3, Lahore'.

In the last thirty years, he continues, there has been a 'big change' in the district. 'Sometimes', he adds, 'I can't believe it.' There have been industrial changes ('small industries have replaced the mills', 'the Ashtonians have been adaptable', and 'the factories are cleaner'), improvements in general health, and immigration. 'Now, there is a large community of Moslems. But they are not westernized Pakistanis who have settled here, not Pakistanis who play cricket.' Nevertheless 'good citizens' in the town have 'tried to enlighten the indigenous population' about the ways of the newcomers. The 'young English', he also claims, 'have left, the older ones remain. The young have become old, and the old decrepit.' Isaacs himself speaks Arabic and Hebrew, Iranian and Kurdish. 'I have also seen a lot of talent wasted in the schools, to feed the factories with semi-skilled labour.' And, something else. 'In the last two or three years, how shall I put it, now you can see again the well-nourished, and – I don't call them ill – the badly nourished.' What do you mean? 'In the older days' what Isaacs describes as the 'lower strata' 'knew how to buy bone and cheap cuts of meat, how to make soup. Now people don't know what you mean when you say a "light diet".' Four of his student contemporaries in Baghdad became generals; another, Abdel-Karim Kassem, became president of Iraq, but was 'bumped off' ('he wasn't a bad fellow, but a depressive').

There have also been, in Ashton, a 'rise in drinking' and 'no abatement of smoking in the lower strata'; 'go to a hospital, the doctor doesn't smoke, but the technicians and porters smoke like chimneys,' he says genially, laughing. 'But they' – the 'lower strata' – 'feel smaller than they used to when I first came

here. The shock of so many unemployed makes a man with a
wife and two children very worried.' People, jobless, become
'inverted, anxious', and 'don't know how to get out of it'; and
if 'too anxious', they 'go on and become depressed, even
psychotic'. Once they get 'sucked into it', he continues, 'you
can't do anything with them. When you show interest in their
skills' – 'a man who has worked in a factory has his own
cleverness' – 'they open up a little. But what they need is
forceful action, or a godsend job, to break the spiral. When the
job centre says to my patient, "We've got something for you",
he will start to smile,' Isaacs says, smiling, 'to dress, to feel
better. I always have to be careful that people don't go from
my surgery, and throw themselves in front of a bus. If I close
the door on a person, and everything becomes black, he might
do something to himself. And if patients have a job, even if
they suffer from prescribed diseases – like byssinosis, or
ectopic allergies from metal-working – I say, "Go back, don't
make a fuss." Better to have an itch and work, than no itch and
no job to go to. In this climate, anyone who gets something
wrong with him can be finished.'

Isaacs has a carefully clipped, pepper-grey moustache and
dark-red bow-tie; is both suave and kindly. 'The percentage
you can blame', he adds, 'is very small.' The employed are
'trying to keep their jobs at all cost'; while the jobless 'want to
work' – although Farrar, in Hyde, had said that 'the skilled
worker just won't go down-market' – 'they are not pessimistic
by nature. The working class is better and more honest than
any other. I never use the word "malingerer". At the DHSS
medical centre, they say to me "this fellow is a parasite", but
these are bad words. They might be lazy, but that is all part of
the character of the British.' ('What I mean really', Isaacs says,
in qualification, 'is they ask for leisure while they work, lazy in
that sense.') 'People know things are bad, they grumble,
they're depressed, but generally they try to accept things. I
look at it objectively,' he goes on, rubbing his chin, 'I wasn't
born here. There is no revolution in their senses. It's amazing,' he adds benignly, 'the monarchy is, we could say,

celebrated, the upper class is – how shall I put it? – rooted. There is no anger,' he adds, smiling. Outside, beyond Azmet Sheikh's white marble minarets, you can see the end-wall of a seedy terrace, half-demolished.

Back in Hyde, at the Clarendon House practice with the women behind the reception counter, opinion is busy and more strident. 'People', one of the dispensers says, 'are wanting more and more, expecting more, not less. They expect it as part of their rights, every little thing. And the people who are greedy, and won't help themselves, are the first to start moaning.' She is a kind person, who calls everyone 'love'; 'if it's lasted three months, love,' she briskly says to an anxious phone-caller, 'it'll last while Monday.' 'The working class', she continues, replacing the receiver, 'know what they can get to the last detail, especially the younger end in their twenties and thirties.' (Dr Farrar disagreed completely: 'The services are there, but the working class don't know it'; 'they make their circumstances fit the bill,' said Livingstone, disagreeing in turn, 'they know what they are doing.') 'They ask for such silly things,' she says, holding out her finger, 'like, "I want my plaster changed." ' 'The dispensers always pile on the agony,' said Livingstone later, calmly. 'They think they're overworked, we think they're overmanned. No hard feelings.'

But she is positively cross, getting quite flushed with it. 'They take it all for granted, they're not ready to help themselves. The people who really need help are the last to call for it. A young lady, in her thirties, came into the surgery the other day to have her nails cut, would you believe it? She said she couldn't do her left hand with the scissors. How ridiculous can you get! She said, "One of you girls can do it." "Oh, give over with you, no, we can't," we told her'; reddening, and getting into a real flummox in the retelling of it. 'We never used to have surgeries like we do these days. We used to be busy in the winters mainly. Now there's no let-up. If it's a cold, they think it's pneumonia; and if it's cotton wool they want, they must have the biggest packet. People are so arrogant, there's just no contentment.' You wouldn't have guessed it. In the waiting-room there are only muted and cautious whispers. Their suffering is in silence, the criticism of them raucous.

'Then', she says, still warming to it, 'there's the blackmail. On the phone they say, "I'll get the doctor out", if you can't get them an appointment when they want it.' (What, these lambs – or sheep – wrapped in their fleeces?) Her kinder, northern self says, 'Some of these patients are a bit cheeky.' 'Quite a number do it,' agrees Dr Livingstone, unruffled. 'They'll call you out for a toothache.' My father used to describe it as a 'wandering fart' in the old days, when doctors did open battle with their patients. Livingstone himself is laconic, mild-mannered. 'I don't think it's any different from what it used to be. You get the minority who'll always complain. They're unbalanced, paranoid or something of the sort,' he says shrugging, dismissive; while people with what he calls 'a known position in the community' – 'mostly the local Labour and trade union people' – 'expect special help. They try to use their positions to get privileges. They pull rank as it were,' he says, without expression.

Behind the counter, with the lid off, emotions are seething, necks flushing, at a 'younger generation' with 'no respect for the doctor'. Unemployment? 'It's terrible, isn't it, but a lot of it's been brought on by sheer greed, less hours, more money'; and 'we're amazed, we all are, at what you can get on the health service. When I first came here I couldn't believe it'; and 'we know all the regulars, oh yes, you can say their addresses off without asking. They say to us, "Do you know my address, love?" ' – relieved laughter breaking out among the pill-boxes of this warfare – 'you have to smile to yourself,' she says, laughing. 'We're a happy little bunch, really,' she goes on, hand absently touching her blouse-collar, 'people in Hyde are very lucky really.'

Yet, as the health service comes under pressure, the whole underlying argument about the nature and purposes of welfare is becoming more intense and more urgent. Moreover, as

Farrar puts it, 'increased dependency on it, in this economic climate, doesn't necessarily mean that people have increased regard for the welfare system'. Beenstock says of the welfare state that 'as an ideal, no one could fault it. But in practice, in an acquisitive society, you can't have people demanding things as of right in an open-ended system. You can't have people calling their holidays "convalescence", or using an ambulance like a taxi.' It is a view from the trenches, of an infantryman under attack from swarms of patients and tired of defending himself with prescriptions and potions. ('In self-defence you have to give them something,' a doctor in Reddish later told me.)

Farrar's priorities seem different. He has been in practice eight years, Beenstock more than twenty. 'The fact that the welfare services are getting worse, and that publicity for them has diminished, is very short-sighted,' Farrar says. Moreover, 'the health of society, as opposed to its sickness, is the major problem. Education and information are crucial.' The health service itself – 'I've never known anything else than the NHS' – is 'not a sacred cow. Mine is a practical assessment. It is simply the best way I can see of working.' He is a socialist, but thinks that 'to legislate private practice out of existence' would be 'totalitarian'. ('The Labour Party', he says, is 'up a blind alley in its opposition to private practice'; 'the people themselves don't give a bugger'.) Instead, Farrar would like to see the health service 'so good that no one wanted to be a private patient'. He adds that the 'true red-hot red dismisses the principle of self-help. But a balanced view has to include it.' 'The first social service', Livingstone says briefly, 'is your friends.' I expect that these voices, between them, constitute the voice of the medical profession. 'And if a doctor gives a patient just consideration, the vast majority will respect him. They may even like him.'

I go out with Livingstone on his visits. A Glaswegian, he started to practise in the area in 1937, went to war, and on VE Day was in Bari. He ended up as a captain anaesthetist in the British hospital in Quetta. The sun is shining, the mills silent, a clean breeze blowing. We are in Newton. It was stale here once, death-grey; ashen, in recollection. There are chrysanthemums in the windows, yellow, white, red-brown, tawny. Most of the sooty privet of wartime has vanished; glue-sniffing is on the increase.

His patient – 'a young girl', he calls her – is forty, and has lung cancer. Her husband ('a good fellow, very supportive') is out of work. I wait in the car. The Edwardian street is deserted. There are small stained-glass swallows in the leaded windows, dark blue, bottle-green, wine-red and yellow-orange. They fly with leaden wings in their jigsaws of coloured glass. These are northern mosaics.

He comes back after only a few minutes, carrying his stethoscope. 'She is dying of it, poor girl,' he says. 'She is very thin, poor thing.' He starts up the engine. The front gardens, low-walled in red brick, are neat and tidy. 'She weeps, she's not very happy about it. She has to work out a philosophy, and wonder why we're here at all,' he says quietly.

Hers is a depression beyond the reach of unemployment, or any prescription. In this street, there is a sudden beauty. It is in the eye of the beholder, thankful for small mercies in the face of terminal disorder. 'To appreciate this kind of thing,' he says, gesturing towards the Pennines, and reading the moment, 'you have to be well.'

Back in the market square, with its stalls and striped red-and-green awnings, the Pakistani stall-holders are putting away their bric-à-brac. There is an acrid smell in the air; the 'Kingston stink', the locals call it.

Once it was the bitter aroma of bodies worked to the bone and picked clean by hardship, the fagged-out fragrance of old clothes and worn-down pavements. Now it is the stench of the local bone-factory, boiling up the carcasses. Round here, you always seem to be sunk in one miasma or another, even when the sun is shining.

Wolverhampton on Ice

December 1981

Birch Street, Wolverhampton, in the icy slush, the wind knifing. On one side of the street is Waring and Gillow ('Where People in the Know Go'); Head-Quarters, the hairdressers; and the Purbani Tandoor restaurant. Hot aromas waver in the freezing snow-flecked cold. On the other side is the dole office, and the dole queue.

Cold has desexed it; the crowd is wrapped, padded and swaddled. In the fag smoke, there are perms under nylon headscarves and young necks in Wolves' colours; turbans and crash-helmets; wellingtons, salwar-and-kameez and ski-pants; saris, cheap coats and black leather jackets, hung with metal and studded. The muffled queue stands, mostly in soaking shoes, in a mulch of slush and chewing-gum wrappers, trampled leaflets and trodden cigarette packets, on the ribbed black-rubber flooring.

'Reception: Please Call Here First' declares a sign; 'Before Claiming, Please Tell the Clerk If You Have Done Any Work Since You Last Claimed Benefit' demands another; 'Under 19? Unemployed? Training Opportunities for YOU with Intercept' offers a third. Names are called out ('M. P. Singh, please!'; 'Arthur Turner!'; 'Frederick Willis!') by stentorian female voices at the counter. Before them, pregnant slatterns stand, smoking, their hair in curlers.

There are family groups, young marrieds, babes in arms, solitary singles; some black, some white, and some grey-blue with cold. There are black faces under tartan caps ('Have you signed on before?'), and Indians in woollen balaclavas ('Have you signed on at any other office?'); premature greyness in polished shoes and mannerly accents; fur-necked anoraks, middle-class suede, and nicotine-stained fingers. It is the great multicultural democracy of the unemployed, lining up beneath the cold strip-lighting for relief in welfare Britain; a

15

latter-day Pilgrim's Progress, from TV set to dole queue, and back again; or a wartime casualty station, with nurses and orderlies on one side of the counter, and patients on the other, in millions.

The queue shuffles slowly forward. At the packed Yew Tree pub, in Merridale – more of a lounge than a tavern – the clusters of pastel turbans bunch over their pint-pots, like tulips. At separate tables the whites, their ale fist-clenched, are supping in their own boozy circles, lip-reading in the din of a suburban bedlam, and grimacing like Brueghel figures. There are 23,583 unemployed in Wolverhampton, 16·1 per cent of the working population; George Grosz would have been at home in this new Weimar.

Jack Jones, an unemployed draughtsman of twenty-seven, did his apprenticeship at Bolton and Paul, and spent five years at Metro-Cammell; he is on the 'professional register' at the job centre. 'On the labour' for two years now, after getting a week's notice, he says, wiping his mouth, that 'you go through three phases when you lose your job'. He has a check shirt, blue-cord jeans, and looks like a student. 'First of all, it's great. I had a bit of money in the bank. I didn't worry too much. That phase lasted a few weeks. Then it hit me: I wasn't going to get a job. Then apathy set in. That phase lasted a while, and then I got desperate.'

The din is increasing; the smoke, eye-smarting. He is getting £19 a week on the dole, of which he gives £10 to his parents with whom he is living, and says that he couldn't marry if he wanted to. 'My friends know I'm out of work. If they're moving house, I'll give them a hand with it, or if they have shelves that need fitting they'll give me a fiver to do it. I can go to a pub and have a couple of pints like now, but I can't go away for a weekend. I have relatives who haven't spoken to me since I was made redundant. A neighbour said to me, "Going to college?" I said, "No." "Where do you work, then?" "I'm not working," I said, "at the moment." He hasn't spoken to me since; we pass in the street, you wouldn't believe it.

'But it's not the stigma that gets to me; it's the financial and social restrictions.' His forehead is shining in the hubbub, gullets gulping around us. 'I'm not a careerist, so I don't feel deprived of an outlet to fulfil my ambitions. On the one hand, I feel it's a waste. I could be doing something socially useful, you know, like making wheelchairs. On the other, once you've been out of work a while, you lose the work habit. In fact, if they paid me more, I wouldn't mind not working. But I try not to think about being thirty or thirty-five in this situation,' he shouts. Being out of work is like doing time; short-term for some, but with life sentences a real prospect for others.

A rage of the mind could blow up in this louring Black Country, growing blacker. 'There'll be trouble round here,' he says. His specs are rimless. 'It's bound to happen. How can you expect people to respect a system that is making them irrelevant, not just redundant? Saying "Give 'em thirty quid a week, they didn't get it in the Thirties" is not an answer.' Why not? 'Because unemployment in Wolverhampton is setting people against each other. Those out of work against those in work. Low-paid in work, against those on benefit getting the same as them. White against black. This is real Powell country. The majority of people take a simplistic view: if you sent them all home, they think there'd be jobs for everybody. The other day, my mother said she'd seen a black man of about eighty shuffling down the road. "What use is he in this country?" she said. I thought, "About the same as you are." '

A drunken and bleary Indian lurches out of the toilets and across the fitted carpets, steadying himself at the Space Invaders, glazed eyes crossing at the winking and pinging targets. Jack himself has 'moved to the left'; both his parents are Tories. 'But a lot of the lads say that "the NF seems to be doing something". Things will be no better if you get rid of the blacks. But the NF give you targets for your anger, and that's going to become more and more important.'

At the job centre in Market Street, Xmas snow dust has been sprayed in white curlicues on the window-panes. 'Disability Can Be Overcome' says a poster: 'Winston Churchill

Had a Speech Impediment.' Cigar-in-mouth, and chin jutting, Churchill stands in the blitz's flaming ruins. The few job cards – for a part-time cook at £1·54 per hour, a 'twenty-eightish' make-up consultant at £63 per week, a gardener-chauffeur 'age forty-five plus' – are wreathed in artificial frost. The two clerks at the desk talk to each other beneath the tinsel.

Shoppers in bootees, struggling with bulging plastic bags and bogged-down push-chairs, slither past the windows. The sky is grey and heavy. Small children, suddenly skidding, get their arms near-yanked from their sockets. 'Wolverhampton HMV Skins', 'Shits' and 'NF' read the city-centre daubs; at the Youth Opportunities Shop, with its stuffed toys and jumble, but no custom, they are collecting 'Parcels for Poland'. 'Heinz Soup', promises the hoarding (beside a car park like a bombsite), 'Will Always Make Things Better.' There are 2,569 under-eighteens on the dole, 2,189 more on temporary job schemes – 'government cheap labour', they call it here. It is going to take more than Heinz soup to sort this lot out.

The plump and pale ex-high-school girl – 'I went to Wolverhampton Girls' High, the posh one,' she says, 'but I failed my A levels instead of becoming a brain surgeon' – has spent two years on the dole herself, and doesn't want her name mentioned, 'or it'll be in the local papers'. She is twenty-three, the daughter of a policeman. 'I've been looking for almost anything; I'd take anything, shop, office. At the start, I got a job as a cashier at a garage, but I was off sick with the flu after three weeks. The doctor told me to stay off a couple of days longer, I was feeling that seedy, but I got the sack for it. In any case, I was expected to kowtow to the manager, and' – chucking herself under her double-chin – 'I wouldn't simper at him either. I wasn't the right sort,' she says grimly. 'I didn't think it would be easy,' she continues, 'but two years was a surprise. I thought I'd get a shop-job at least. But I didn't get a shop-job either.' (Nor, evidently, did the thin skinhead, with the delicate bony fingers, scribbling at mid-morning on the condensation of the bus-shelter window. 'I was ere. I rule' he was tracing. He had a black crombie and hobnail boots, with a Union Jack transfer at the ankle.)

She disapproves 'strongly' of all government-funded make-work schemes ('I forget what all the letters, MSC, YOP, STEP and the rest of it stand for,' she says, laughing). She calls it 'exploiting the kids, doing people out of a job' – 'what they say is, "Let's sack Bill, and get a kid in to do it" ' – 'and paying them next to nothing'. According to her, 'it's only in theory a training. In practice, there isn't the money to employ more people.'

'We'll be going back to assassination soon,' she adds, giggling. Assassination? 'The only way to get a job,' laughing again. 'People have stopped thinking they'll get jobs now in Wolverhampton. In fact, they're leaving school expecting not to get a job. They haven't stopped trying, but they've stopped *thinking* they'll get one. You can't blame them, when it's getting more unusual for a kid to have a job round here, than not to have one. A lad I know is joining the Marines. He's not the sort, it's tragic, but what else is there? They just go through the motions, knowing they're not going to get anything. Not many of them blame themselves, or get blamed by their parents.' (But in the Wolverhampton Education Department, they say that the young unemployed 'begin to feel there's something wrong with them'.) 'A lot of them get depressed, but some who just accept it can be fairly cheerful. You hear them joking, "A job? What's a job?" If people were starving to death it might be different. Apart from hating Thatcher' – 'even a lot of the little kids think Thatcher's a baddie' – 'they don't know who to blame. They feel anger, but it's not directed. It's very personal, nothing coherent. Most of them aren't political at all, not even slightly. A few might say, "They've got us on the dole, now they want to blow us to oblivion", but not many.' And racism? 'There's a lot of racism about. But many of the younger ones, ten to twelve years old, are only racist because their parents are. A lot of the young blacks themselves are so apathetic that they don't even take racism seriously. It's amazing to me having to convince a

young black girl, can you believe it, that the National Front
was a bad idea. Most of the unemployed black lads are
religious, mainly Jehovah's Witnesses, or Rastas. They've
been brought up religious, so they're more into it. And all the
cut-backs', she says, 'are making religion more and more
important to them. They feel some sort of support from it' –
'aaagh, the arguments,' she adds, clutching her head and
laughing again. 'They wander around a lot, like the whites,
gradually losing touch with those who are working. They go to
the adventure playground, hang around outside the chip shop,
go to the discos at the Poly. You can see them all over.'

Christine Atherton, a maths teacher at Barr Beacon Comprehensive, seven years into teaching, agrees. 'I see a lot of
kids in town I've taught, just walking around. I find it
increasingly difficult to say to them in lessons, "This is going
to be useful to you when you get a job", when I know it isn't,
when I can see their potential is going to be wasted. It's
heartbreaking to hear some of them say to you, "My dad is
going to get me a job, miss", when you know they're dreaming.' Now, she has these two Christmas weeks for recuperation
('teachers don't like being in this situation'), before going back
into the front-line's trenches; 'there's nothing waiting for
them, we've failed them'. There is a total of eight registered
job vacancies for young people in Wolverhampton.

There were roaring steel mills around here once, infernos of
molten lava and sweating labour. Alongside the Wolverhampton to Birmingham Road, at Bilston, at Sedgley and many
other places, they lie now like beached hulks, skeletal, silent
and blackened. We are in one of the breakers' yards of British
skill and labour, abandoned to the auctioneers, the demolition
gangs and the vandals. Bernard Foley is a skilled furnace
bricklayer. He is thirty-three, son of a steel-worker. He tolls
the places off on his fingers: Rubery Owen at Darlaston
('That's gone now'), Church and Bramhall's ('They're having
a rough time'), Charles Richards ('They finish Friday'). He
worked at Stewart's and Lloyds at Bilston, and lost his job
there in November 1980.

'Factory after factory I see closed and up for sale,' he says, 'just in the space of a mile. They're defacing whole communities, not just individuals.' Defacing? 'Yes, defacing.' His front room with its pebble-glass panes in the bow windows, has thick-pile red carpet, deep red wallpaper, and a red telephone. We are in Willenhall. The wingback chairs are blue and red plush-velvet. A lot of his £9,750 redundancy money – seventy-eight weeks' pay at 90 per cent of his last earnings – has gone into this décor; many of the 'older folk', in a workforce of 5,300, had been 'labouring at Stewart's since they were kiddies. Some of those blokes I worked with I really loved. They severed a relationship, like someone taking a loved one from me. It was seventeen years of my life. All that just took away, wiped away in a week or a fortnight. They severed the lot.' With the severance pay, he bought a car, a 'breakfast bar', a colour television 'for the kids', and 'this unit'. It is a large farmhouse-style dresser: 'what Jacqueline wanted' – she works part-time at Marks and Spencer – with leaded windows.

After he had lost his job – 'when someone says your skill is not needed' – he had been made to feel 'like a leper, an outcast. They label you as a scrounger when you lose your status. It's degrading.' He has found a temporary job, but it is 'just working from day to day', with unemployment 'always tagging along behind me'. In addition, at the dole-office counter, there are what he calls 'them people of my own age looking down on me. They say they don't, but they do. You can see it in their faces. It's just "Come back in a fortnight". We don't spend enough time on individuals, person to person, not three hundred in a dole queue.' Once upon a time, 'the different firms used to send to the schools for machine-workers, electricians, carpenters, bricklayers'. But that was all of twenty years ago. As a lad of fifteen, when he had first gone into the steel mill as an apprentice, it had been 'all activity, gatherings of people. When I came out of my time, I was relying on my skill, I thought that was it, set up, made for life,' he continues. 'I never thought about the economic situation of the country as a whole. You could book your holidays for next year and say, "In three years' time, I'll buy a car." ' Now, the old place is a black hulk, with its fires extinguished; it had been, then, 'a brand-new world, all sparks; it was brilliant. I'd go back,' he says, 'if they opened it up tomorrow.'

By 1976, he continues, 'we realized no investment was coming in to Bilston. We thought it was deliberate, but you couldn't get to the bottom of it; though we didn't think the place would shut down completely. "Don't worry," they used to say, as if they were joking, "we'll give you enough money to buy yourselves a cottage in the country." We believed they'd never get away with it, that it was for the generations that were going to come in the future. We had a livelihood from it. But the inheritance', as he puts it, 'has gone for ever. When it happened, it knocked me for six. It made me angry as well.' Why? 'Because no one was coming up to learn the skills I'd learned. I felt all those years had been wasted.' His wife – whose father has recently lost his job at British Leyland, and 'had his whole life shattered' into 'a nervous breakdown' – 'used to say "summat'll turn up". But it was like being in hell, I'd had such a happy time there. I used to just sit and have a cry on my own' – 'exploding in my privacy' and 'blowing up very quickly', he calls it – 'I was so depressed. I couldn't even stand the kiddies. I've never been contented since I left. It was a great hole for me, what with all the things you take for granted, when you've been used to working, when you've been used to a certain standard of living.' Together with the redundancy-velvet, there are reproduction wheelbacks, the Christmas tree is present-hung, and the large lampshade is made of wicker.

He declares that 'it's the government's obligation to keep up that standard of living', and that 'we ought to be a thriving nation. It wants', he says, 'summat drastic doing with the country. We have to have a deep think about the set-up of the country, to make it more even. I'm more politically minded now. I detest the Tories, I absolutely detest them. Before, you thought you were settled, and didn't look to the problems of other people. What's happened to me has made me more caring, because there are thousands of us. It wants us going out on the streets, to get them to listen to the cry of the people.' He can see 'no hope' for his kids; 'it's degrading to say you need O levels and A levels, and at the end of it, nothing. You have your little dreams and fancies about the children, and you see them shatter. When I was at school, I had hopes. But, for them, what is there?'

He has friends who are 'scared now, they're going right'; 'blaming it on Benn, saying, "It's him who's doing away with the Labour Party", and "It's not worth having those policies of his and no Labour Party in the finish." ' He himself is 'more Wedgie Benn' than he's ever been. He used to be 'more central, more give-and-take'. And what about fascism? 'Hitler brought his country out of depression. What he did was marvellous, until he began rampaging, hating the Jews and all that.' The room is a blood-red haze, as red as the ruins in the Churchill poster; and, with the heat at full blast, as hot as a furnace.

Back in town, up to its ankles in lead-grey slurry, you can hear of a new 'People's Centre' in the making. A by-product of the People's March for Jobs, which came through Wolverhampton in May 1981, the planning for it has taken wing. The TUC had recommended setting up 'unemployment centres'. A local group of community workers, teachers, a DHSS officer, a librarian and trade union activists (led by John Clifford, an organiser with the building union UCATT, and seconded full-time to the project), thought differently. 'I wasn't happy about it,' says Clifford, 'when I heard it being talked about in the UCATT office. You have to think about a lot more things than just unemployment. "We'll harness the unemployed," they were saying. But we wanted to get away from the soup-kitchen approach of the 1930s', and from what he calls 'the stigma of the Thirties' Youth Clubs'. In Clifford's opinion, 'getting welfare today is not much different from then, mainly hand-outs'; while the unemployed in Wolverhampton themselves are 'tolerated, but little more' in the town's existing community centres. 'Something new' was needed, according to Clifford: 'we didn't want a special place for unemployed people, as if they were a separate alien minority. You have to have the employed involved too, which includes those facing short-time, redundancy and lay-offs. We want a place where unemployed and employed can work together.'

The result is the plan for the People's Centre – 'there is nothing like it at all anywhere in the country' – which has got the cautious, or reluctant, backing of the local authority. 'We've been accused by the Socialist Workers' Party of being a tea-and-sympathy organization,' says Clifford. Volunteer fund-raising events have included a 'sponsored barge-haul', a dog-show and a skittle evening ('I'm quite prepared to have a pigeon-show, if that will attract people'); culminating in a packed disco on the night of the Toxteth riots. 'We have to tread carefully, because we need wide support from the churches, the chamber of commerce, and even the Conservative group in council. We want the idea to mushroom, because it is socially good, and so as those who won't help, won't hinder.' The People's Centre is ultimately intended to provide welfare counselling – 'not just "We'll get you three pounds a week extra, mate" ' – an information centre, education classes, entertainment and arts facilities, a bookshop, a law centre, a printing press and even the means for co-operative production ('things they can make, things they can sell'), with a staff of eighty.

Yet, isn't all this just a 'socialist' form of welfare? 'Yes, in the short term,' says young Ian Philips, one of the Centre's putative organizers, and an 'outreach officer' in Wolverhampton Education Department's 'Careers Service'. He has crinkly fair hair and long fingernails; is dressed in black jacket, jeans and brown roll-neck sweater. His official brief, in working hours, is to 'work with the alienated young unemployed' – 'alienated youth is the label, it transfers the blame from society to them' – and to 'get them back into the system'. But, he declares direly, 'the facilities are inadequate; the youth, many of whom have older sisters and brothers, as well as fathers and mothers, on the dole, are not interested; and, to tell you the truth, the employment services are not all that interested in them either.' Are you joking? 'It's all form-filling, hassles, production-line queuing for hours, not enough personal attention. And in the end they can't get them a job. They can go for a welding course, but they won't get a job as a welder.' His beard is blond and wispy. 'A year ago, two years ago,' he continues, 'most of my conversations with eighteen- and nineteen-year-olds were about employment. Now they're about what they're into, encouraging them to get into self-help projects, to look at their skills in a different way – not directly related to "a job" – and to see themselves as valuable people.'

That's why, claim Clifford and Philips, their 'Wolverhampton People's Centre' ('it will be open twenty-four hours a day if they want it') is needed. 'Unlike the existing welfare system,' says Philips, 'because its growth will depend on the people themselves and will bring out their talents, it will be a vibrant place.' It will be, says Clifford, a 'living organism', in a dying landscape.

There are thus two themes in their conversation, in the front room of Clifford's semi in Oxley, hung with Xmas bunting, and with a plate of mince-pies on the table. (In a cage stands a silent canary; 'he can talk canary, he can,' someone says admiringly of Clifford, as the bird suddenly comes to life to his expert susurrations.) One theme is the 'untapped talents of the dole queue, talents which can be used for the community's benefit, if we can get them to think differently about themselves'. ('It looks like apathy to the outsider, but it's lack of self-belief, really.') The other theme is 'what people call leisure time', in a society which will never again see full employment. 'We've just got to come to terms with the technological revolution. Unemployment is part of the problem of our time,' says Clifford. In school, continues Philips – 'where', he adds (as if it were absurd), 'they are still educating for a job' – 'kids are taught that only going to the factory is work. But there are other kinds of work. For example, what you call leisure activities, we look at as work activities' – creative self-help activity, above all. 'Moreover, there are so many practical jobs that need doing. And if you're the man who repairs all the cars in the street, you'll have standing. A can give B £10 to do the guttering, B gives C £10 to repair his car, C gives D £10 to do this, that or the other, and so it goes,' says Philips, laughing.

Clifford, a former building worker, ex-Ruskin student and son of a railwayman – 'he worked shifts all his life, his social life was nothing' – considers the People's Centre, which will promote such activity, to be 'the beginning of a movement'; more precisely, in the light of what he calls his 'political thoughts' and 'study of the past', Clifford sees the Centre as 'a microcosm of what the labour movement is supposed to be. This is the sort of thing the trade union movement should be doing.' (But there is not a cat-in-hell's – nor a dreamer at the Tammany bargaining table's – chance of it.) He says the trade unions should stop arguing about jobs as if they were 'personal possessions'. They belong to the community; 'only if the community decides, should a job go'. And though the job may become redundant, 'the individual who does it, never'. He even speaks – in this unlikely setting for a new utopia, or a new New Lanark – of 'reawakened people, learning at the Centre to take an interest in their own physical environment, or working full-time at music or silk-screen printing', and sounds like a latter-day William Morris. 'With this philosophy, and developing this side of culture,' he says, 'it should go on for ever. But I've been frightened to say too much,' he adds anxiously, 'in case I got laughed out of court.' 'He wants to change the world, does John,' says his girlfriend, admiring. 'I want to put up a mirror, so that people can take a look at themselves,' says Clifford.

Confident again over tea mugs, they talk in a homely, warm cocoon, criss-crossed with tinsel, the black cat on the floral carpet eyeing the canary, their dream a world away from the frozen lives being lived in this frigid Valhalla; where time itself is coming to be measured less by the rhythm of human activity, than by the calendar months and years, by the stasis, of unemployment. An 'alternative economy', a 'second economy' – 'built up on encouraging self-help and the development of individual skills' – 'could be based on our philosophy in Wolverhampton,' says Philips.

I go with them to the estate agent, where they are negotiating for city centre premises for their project. Crumpled jeans and beards face up to the aftershave and dark blue pinstripe. The office is all reproduction Regency, with more veneer than polish; outside, it has begun an icy downpour. The agent looks like Mickey Rooney – or Sir Michael Edwards – with an accent like a saw-mill, and cuff-links like pigeon's eggs. Behind this shored-up façade, how deep an abyss is there?

Shooting his cuffs, he says, 'I'm much in favour of your movement. Get ahead and do it quick. I meet people out of work all the time. They come in here with £5,000 redundancy money, want to start a new business, but haven't a clue what to do with it. The idea is super.' But the asking rent for the People's Centre is £6,000 per annum.

Something had better happen soon in Wolverhampton, that's for certain. 'If a person ask me, what hope have I got and why am I living?' says Tony Webster, a quiet twenty-one-year-old West Indian, 'I can say that I have a religion.' Out of work for two years, he has three CSEs in Building Development, Humanities and Art – 'we had drilled in us, "work hard, pass exams, get a job"' – from Wardesley Comprehensive. (His father, after twenty-five years as a Wolverhampton bus conductor, is unemployed also.) When he went for a job at Bilston Street metal works, 'I was asked', he says softly, 'if I was a street-fighter.' He had six months' youth employment, 'and after, I had to move on, looking and looking. I found a crummy Indian place at Fox Lane, the C and B Brass Polishing Company, machining brass handles for very low wages. It was dirty,' he says, talking intensely, like a black Gorky, of his apprenticeship to life, 'but I was prepared to stick it out. The place was suddenly taken over by other Asians; I was left in the dark, perhaps because I was a West

Indian. The new boss started getting rough with me, saying I wasn't making enough effort. I complained to my parents; they saw that I was being unjustly treated. I left after four months. Like other youngsters, I never thought what I wanted to do. I didn't look ahead, I didn't foresee what was going to happen, I just lived day-by-day, like all the others.' Today the whole family is ready for the Second Coming. 'Jehovah', he says, 'is going to intervene to put things right. He will not let man destroy the world. I have faith in the Bible. I know what I can expect in the future.'

God, not the job centre, will find work for Wolverhampton? He brushes the question away. 'I know something unpleasant is going to happen,' he says, placid. 'I'm not rebellious, but in the last two years, I've been seeing a lot of things. People fighting, hitting people on the streets in Wolverhampton for no apparent reason. I can see things building up. If I hadn't been a Jehovah's Witness, preaching God's Kingdom, I couldn't have stuck up to being unemployed myself, I'd have gone berserk. I'd have been doing the same thing as I saw all of them doing. I can see the youngsters, black and white, the look on their faces. These are the signs of the last days'; or Messianic moments in the Black Country. He speaks gently, and has a weak, pliant handshake at parting. 'This is Satan's system,' he declares, 'and he has turned the world upside-down. I know that we are in the last days now.' In the meantime, he is playing a policeman in the Zip Theatre Company's production of *Mother Goose*, a make-work theatre project. These are mad, mad days, my masters; for, after *Mother Goose*, Tony Webster will be appearing in the dole queue, until the Last Judgment.

Archie Howells ('the longest I'd been out of work before, since leaving school, was four weeks') is sitting in front of his artificial coal-fire in carpet slippers. An ex-miner, who originally came down from Kilmarnock to work at the local Sedgley colliery, he is in no mood to wait for anything. 'I feel angry, very angry,' he says, getting up to switch off the 3 p.m. television. 'I thought I'd be out of work for a couple of months at the most,' he says, bitter, his voice abrasive, 'but now I can see no end to it. It gets on your nerves, decorating the house, watching television, it gets you down.' Preoccupied ('I'm worried about this country,' he says), lined and grey, he is getting £40 a week on the dole. A 'survival-kit', he calls it. (The 'only solution' is 'getting Mrs Thatcher on the dole. It's Tory policy to keep us hungry,' he exclaims fiercely.) The rent is £22 a week. 'I'm down to twenty a day now,' he says, of the cigarette in his hand, 'and that's my one bloody pleasure. The pub looks packed on a Saturday night, but you just watch what people are drinking. Two pints is the limit. They don't give you no spending money on "the labour",' he says, grinning, or grimacing. His Scots-flint voice, in the cold room, strikes harshly. He became a steelworker at Redman and Fisher, when he lost his job at Sedgley; and that job, too, went under. In May 1981, he 'finished'.

'The government', he adds sourly, 'has killed the working man, and ruined the country. As long as that woman is there, it's got no future.' In addition, the unions are 'losing their strength'; 'old people' are 'blaming the blacks' – 'but it's about time we started looking after our own,' he says, coughing; and he 'can see no future' for his children. There is no sweetness-and-light here; only spleen-and-bile, and heavy smoking. 'I went to see about a job this morning. They don't want to know. There are no jobs to be got round here. You can call it a ghost-town,' he adds, gesturing at my notebook. He says that he can only live for another couple of months on what's left of his redundancy money; he has already 'done without' a holiday last year. ('I'd have been worse off now, if I'd spent it.') 'Once upon a time, you could get jobs if you moved. But those days are over. And what chance has a man of forty-five' – he seems much older – 'got of finding employment? Eh? I ask you,' he demands, 'what chance is there? Everywhere you go, there are no vacancies. Most men would do anything to get a job,' he says, again coughing, 'but you can't get one.'

His son is unemployed too. Only eighteen, he had worked at a local steel rolling mill for eleven months, before himself becoming redundant. 'The lad himself doesn't think he's got a future. He's probably up at the club playing pool at the moment. He knows there's nothing for him. All they do is roam the streets. And when the young lads go for jobs, the first thing they ask them is, "What experience have you got?" It's all wrong. It even costs two pounds to go to the pictures. You can take it from me,' he says, 'there is no future for anyone round here at all.' A large stuffed dog – a shaggy-nylon borzoi – and an inflated-rubber Father Christmas stand together in the room's corner, beside the small Christmas tree. We are in a Coseley council house. The sofa is upholstered in a fur of black nylon. 'He has really given up, he's had enough.' At eighteen? 'At eighteen, nineteen next birthday.' The room suddenly seems colder; the fire all light and no heat, switched on only for decoration; his anger, too, cold, without fire. 'If a Tory comes knocking at my door,' he says, 'I'd smack him round the mouth.' The mood is hard and ugly.

Two doors away – many in the quiet cul-de-sac are unemployed – is Ray Dawes, a man of thirty-three, a moulder for eight years, out of work for two, and gone to get the shopping. Bean's, the engine-makers, where he worked, was taken over and then shut down by British Leyland. On a shelf are heaps of books, plants, a Charles-and-Di coffee mug, and a man-o'-war inside a thin bottle; a well-hung Christmas tree, and a cassette recorder. Ray Dawes's wife says that it is three months since her husband even bothered to go to the job centre. ('He used to go every week, but he's given up now. You get these rumours that things are starting up. When you look round, they have a few cards at the job centre, but they're only offering you a pittance.') Her father, fifty-two and himself redundant, was a tool-setter 'at Wolverhampton Screw and Rivet'; her mother works part time as a cleaner.

'I've cut down with myself a lot,' she says, her fingernails close-bitten. 'Clothes and hair mainly. I used to have it done every Friday or Saturday, washed and set, ready for the weekend. In the last twelve months, I've had two new dresses: one on my birthday, when my Mum and Dad gave me the money, and this Christmas. I get really upset sometimes, really angry.' Why? 'Any woman wants to look nice for her husband,' she answers, plucking at an invisible blemish on her furry jumper. 'When he comes home at night, you make yourself look nice for him. It doesn't make such a difference,' she says, smoothing her skirt, 'not now it doesn't. Even the dog' – a large Afghan – 'has come down from his tin-and-a-half of Chum, to a tin of summat cheaper. He's an expense we can't afford, but he's the kids' pet, so what can we do about it?' The young children, Brett and Kelly, are playing on the floor, painting. 'I still have a cig though, I like me smoke, don't I, Kelly?' she says – accent suddenly broadening – to her small, silent daughter, who sits tongue between teeth with concentration.

The rented colour TV is on, but soundless. 'I was lucky when I was a kid,' she continues, 'I can see it now. My father had a trade. He was always working. They never seemed to struggle, not like we do.' There are polished brass ornaments and a stone beer-jar; the gas-fire in the hearth flares in the awkward silence, as she waits for her husband. 'When a bloke's at work,' she says demurely, 'you look forward to him coming home at teatime. When you're together all day, it isn't the same, is it? We get on each other's nerves; he's sitting about, we bicker.' There is a canary in one cage, and a couple of budgies in the other. 'They need a job,' she adds, 'to keep their minds occupied, don't they?' On the big coloured screen, cartoon mouths open and close in a fish-tank silence. 'He does a lot of reading, though, does Ray, I'll say that for him, goes to the library for his cowboy stories. And he likes a bit of decorating.' (Roy told me later that he preferred horror stories. 'There's always someone in them worse off than me, that's why I read them,' he said, laughing.)

The room is warm and well-kept; she, neatly dressed, hair shining. 'This is the second Christmas on his redundancy money. We can hang on another twelve months, no longer. I've not cut down on the food yet. My kids' – she says that they ask Ray, 'Why don't you work any more, Daddy?' – 'have the

best of what I can afford.' What do you mean? 'They don't go
without, but now I have to look around, and find something
cheaper. Things like shoes. I always used to have their feet
measured, and get proper Clarks for them, but now I can't do
it.' There is a sound of paint brushes in a tin-mug, rattling. 'If
it had been as bad as this a few years ago, I'd never have had
them, not for them to start going short, I wouldn't. What's
going to happen to my two?' The coloured shadows on this
cave-wall have begun to chase each other.

'The future looks black to me,' she says. 'It worries me with
the bills that much, that we worry every time we put the lights
on. You can't pay for it out of the dole money, you have to
keep drawing on the redundancy. There's always people
worse' – 'look at Poland,' she added – 'but I keep telling Ray
the redundancy's not lasting.' The rent and rates come to
£44·60 a fortnight. 'Last year, the week at Rhyl went. I said to
Ray, "We'll cut down on day trips, zoos and such like for
them, it'll come in handy at Christmas", plus the money their
grandad gives the babbies for their presents.' When he comes
in, Ray ('I'm for the SDP, I am') turns out to be raffish, with
owlish eyes, a drooping Edwardian moustache and a gold
ear-ring. He is carrying his library books, bound in plastic
('He must have read the whole library by now,' says his wife,
relaxing). 'There's no pleasure on the dole,' he says, exhaling
and sitting down, 'forty-four pence a pint and fourteen bloody
pubs shutting. You can laugh,' he says – his wife not laughing.
He gets up again, restless and quickly souring. 'There's no
bloody pleasure, no bloody nothing. The bloody country's
wrecked.' Why? 'Too many Indians,' he says without expression. 'And they're still letting them in,' his voice pinched and
nasal. 'They come over here and go on the social, or they're
doing jobs which the English could be doing. They've been
here so bloody long, some of them, that you can't send 'em
back where they came from.' A moment later he refers to
'those riots at Brixton'. 'I'd send 'em home,' he says flatly, 'all
them darkies.' His wife, awkward again in the sudden silence,
gnaws at a fingernail, frowning. 'You're prejudiced,' she says

softly, the budgie chirping. 'Ninety per cent of these looters',
says Ray, 'are darkies.'

But then she herself thinks, without being asked, that
Enoch Powell is 'great'. 'He's the man to rule this country,' she
says, a Labour supporter and voter. (She also believes that
'they should bring back hanging. I think if they had hanging,
or standing them up against the wall and shooting them,
they'd think twice about mugging.') 'He'd make a great prime
minister, would Enoch. Ten years ago,' she says, warming –
or flushing – and sitting forward on the sofa, 'he forecast all
this about the dark people. And it's all come to the truth,
hasn't it?' Ray, however, says that the Tories are 'no bloody
good and Labour's no better' – 'they am,' says his wife, in
broad West Midlands, 'Thatcher'll end up being assassinated'
– 'fighting between each other, no future plans and all this
nationalization. We want', says Ray, 'a straightforward, honest
government which will do the things that need doing. The
NF', he continues, 'is coming up. I imagine them getting
stronger, I do. The NF's got some good points,' he says in a
confidential undertone, 'but I don't like the way they want to
go about it.' 'He's got some funny ideas,' says his wife, uneasy
at my notebook. 'No, I haven't,' says Ray, 'I don't think I'm
biased. I don't want to see them starved and beaten, like Hitler
done,' he says. 'I'm not against blacks altogether. I've worked
with 'em. But what I think about them is what the majority
think.' The canary begins to sing for the first time. 'All I want
is a good house and a good living.' 'All he wants is a job,' says
his wife, by way of correction.

On the doorstep, he tells me that he hopes 'the miners go on
strike' and 'fetch her out, like they did with Heath'. 'Next
time,' he adds, 'I think I'll be voting Labour.' (So this is the
floating voter.) 'Where can I get what you'll be writing?' he
asks meekly. *New Society*. 'What's that then?' A weekly paper.
'Where can you buy it?' At W. H. Smith. 'That's owned
by Jews, did you know that?' he says, taking me by the elbow.

Outside, it is all black ice; and on a surface like this, who
can keep his balance?

Socialism, in One City

January 1983

From the balcony of 'red' Sheffield's besieged town hall –
'fighting' to keep up services and keep down rate increases,
and with £50 million already lost in government grants and
subsidies – Whitehall seems to be closing in on the city. You
need to be a war correspondent to do justice to some of the
battlefield rhetoric, in which surcharges and reserve powers
have become the local government equivalents of MX missiles; or a Clausewitz, to write up these 'grass-roots' war-
games.

The town hall itself, Sheffield's Gothic Winter Palace, has
stone corridors and shining baronial woodwork; a beleaguered
last redoubt from which to 'defend Sheffield' (technically only
a district within the metropolitan county of South Yorkshire)
against the 'biggest attack for half a century on working
people'. For fifty-six years – with the exceptions of 1933 and
1968 – a Labour bastion, Sheffield now faces a new wave of
'savage' spending cuts, which the city reckons could cost it up
to another £24 million.

John Osborn, the only Tory MP in South Yorkshire, sees
himself as 'carrying the flag' in a 'red mire', no less. And with a
dog lead on his desk, and a black Labrador asleep under it,
David Blunkett, the blind thirty-five-year-old Barnsley technical college lecturer, and leader of the town hall's Labour
forces – who went to Sheffield University after a youthful stint
of clerical 'dogsbodying' at the local Gas Board – appeals, like
any de Gaulle, for 'vision' and 'courage', after 'generations of
struggle'. With sixty of the city council's eighty-seven seats
behind him, Blunkett is well dug in across the centre. And
Labour are similarly impregnable in the South Yorkshire
metro county. Yet a battle is under way, Blunkett says,
looking askance, to 'determine our destiny' and to 'defend our
city'. These days, political hyperbole knows no boundaries.

And, on my right, over in the Charter Square coffee lounge
of the Grosvenor (Trust House Forte's plate-glass embassy in
Britain's mythical 'socialist republic of South Yorkshire'), is
businessman Irvine Patnick, OBE, the fifty-two-year-old Conservative opposition leader on the South Yorkshire county
council. Dressed for the struggle in black polo-neck, tailored
black slacks, moccasins and silver bracelet, he declares that
'the faster they knock me down, the quicker I come back. If
they want to brawl in the streets and kick, I'll kick with them.
When they say, "I had to cross a yard to go to the toilet", I say,
"So did I." I went to school with most of them. The only
difference between us is that we put a sink in our house before
they did.' He describes himself as 'more politically aware than
most'; and adds, by way of explanation, that he has read the
Communist Manifesto to 'see what makes the buggers tick'.

We should stay with him for a moment. For he has a long
point-by-point indictment of Sheffield Labour, a demonology
which he is 'going to get published', spread across his knees
like a field commander's order of battle – 'it's called doing your
homework, this' – and painstakingly written out in red and
blue capital letters. His 'speaking notes', he calls them. 'Last
year,' he reads, in gold-rimmed specs, 'they put up a red flag
on the town hall on May Day. They object to the existing
regime in Chile, and the way Allende was ousted. They gave
the facilities of Sheffield to a CND conference, and charged
them nothing for it. They object to selling council houses.
They fund left organizations. They've declared Sheffield a
nuclear-free zone and a peace city'; it is plainly the left's long
retreat from reason. 'They refuse to conform with government
policy on pay, prices and rent increases. They send out
political propaganda with the rate demands.' (To turn the
page, he licks his index-finger.) 'They're against civil defence.
They use the rates to make political appointments. They've
refused to apply for a local enterprise zone. They say to us, "If
you want cuts, we'll impose them in Tory areas only." They
won't stand for the loyal toast,' he reads, shaking his head in
disbelief. 'They support anti-blood-sports campaigning. They

call the Lord Mayor' – 'for me, he represents the Queen' –
"Comrade chairman". And they've chosen my ward for the
only gipsy encampment in the area.' He looks up from his
well-thumbed text. 'This,' he says tersely, 'is not a normal
city.'

Irvine Patnick's parents were 'second-hand dealers in junk'
('Father used to buy,' he says, with a strange relish, 'and
Mother to sell'), who 'made Steptoe look respectable and
decent'; 'I ought to have been a socialist with my background.'
The Sheffield *Star* calls him a 'flamboyant Tory', and a 'Tory
character', with a 'no-frills, grass-roots South Yorkshire style'.
He calls himself a 'scourge of socialism', and says that he is
'made out to be a monster', but that there are 'plenty of beasts
like me around the country'. He is wearing some kind of
perfumed aftershave, and says, like a gloomy Napoleon on
Elba, suddenly despairing, that 'the people of Sheffield are
absolutely lost'. Lost? 'Yes, lost. this is more or less a
communist city. The old Labour guard has been ousted. The
far-leftists, the reds, have taken over.'

In search of the left flank, such as it is, of the class struggle,
a subsidized 5p bus ride across the city will bring you to the
Duke Street Trades and Labour Club. Here, among the
lunchtime drinkers, you will find a member – I mean a
supporter – of Militant; there aren't many in Sheffield,
'between thirty and forty'. Mike Smith, a young South
Yorkshire county councillor with a pint of Mansfield's in one
hand, a fag in the other, and the *Guardian* on the bench
beside him, thinks the town hall, despite 'some of the most
progressive policies in the country', is dominated by 'com-
promisers' and 'left reformists'. 'There are', he declares, jar to
his lips, 'too many professional people in the Labour hier-
archy, too many careerists and opportunists', who 'don't know
what working-class roots are all about'. He himself worked as
an export clerk in a steel mill; 'I try to bring in the common-
or-garden, rank-and-file workers.' Blunkett, for whom he
professes admiration, he describes (perceptively) as 'a very
cautious fellow'. 'I get my politics', he continues – on behalf of

the inner party opposition – 'from working-class people. I'm with the working class all day and every day. I soak up all their influences,' he says, draining his glass, 'their worries and aspirations. They're happier talking to me in my lingo. I raise a series of demands, the same way as Trotsky raised demands, to take the working class forward.' Himself a member of the county police committee, his present battlefield position is 'like Trotsky's at Brest-Litovsk'. The tipple flows without a hiccup. 'He said, "No peace, no war". My slogan is the same.' The same? 'No loss of services, and no rate increases. The balloon will go up, if we keep passing it on to the ratepayer.'

There are obviously military tacticians of struggle and counter-struggle from one end of this besieged city to the other. Patnick, Smith says, is 'a Jew' (but then so was Lev Davidovich Bronstein, alias Leon Trotsky), 'whose parents bought clothes that the working class throws away'; he is a 'rags to riches businessman' and 'local stooge of Thatcher', who 'loves the capitalist system which gives him a living. Most of the other council Tories in Sheffield', he adds, 'are sales reps, garage owners, shopkeepers, that kind of thing. The days of the rich steel barons on the council – the Firths, the Browns, the Osborns – are over. Wealthwise, Patnick is the biggest.'

And, in turn, according to Sid Cordle – 'hissing Sid', the nasty Labour lads call him – a 'new breed of leftists' has 'clear supremacy' in the politics of Sheffield. 'Fairly squarely behind Margaret Thatcher', he is the new twenty-seven-year-old Tory councillor for Eccleshall, and sells insurance for the Prudential. Fidgeting, he says he has a 'strong Christian background' and a 'hatred of communism', which has 'riddled' the local Labour Party. 'I see myself', he declares, 'as counteracting the left-wingers, coming in with the same background and seeking to use the same tactics, to fight socialism and Marxist propaganda. I stand for a loving and caring society,' he says, closing his eyes, 'and good morals.' The son of a council rent-collector from Reading ('I wouldn't call myself working class'), with a trim moustache, a BA in Biblical Studies, and constantly twisting his fingers, Cordle has read both the *Communist Manifesto* and Ralph Miliband: 'an intensely Marxist writer,' he says darkly. Sheffield's new Labour 'strategists', like Blunkett – 'cool, calculated and clever' – are 'well equipped with degrees, study all the time, Open University and that sort of thing', and, the young man from the Pru reckons, are bent 'not just on making Sheffield left-wing, but on helping to overturn the capitalist system'. Worse still, Conservative central office has 'given up Sheffield as a no-hope area'. That is, something like revolution, or the end of the world, is staring sturdy Sheffield (and also Ken Livingstone's Greater London) in the face, hurrying its 560,000 unwitting citizens towards a Marxist Armageddon.

Out in the city, grey on grey, there is not even a trace of 'red mire', and not a barricade or bunker; 'built like Rome on seven hills', according to the lyric official handbook, but with the wind nipping and gusting down from the moors; stubborn to a fault, and home to both the NUM headquarters and the Manpower Services Commission; and with not a sign of apocalyptic fever in its 'pedestrianized precincts'. They haven't even had a good riot, no Brixton or Toxteth, no twentieth-century Sheffield outrages, despite the city's 43,000 unemployed – up in three years from 16,000 – and running at a rate of 30 per cent, or over, on some of the worst-hit council estates.

'Restructuring the manufacturing base', the Tories call the unmaking of Sheffield. 'Decimation' is the Labour term for it. 'Gone are the dark industrial skies of yesteryear,' sings the Promotion Committee's hand-out; going, or gone, much of the industrial activity which produced them. The steel mills are closing, the furnaces falling silent, the cutlery industry being cut to pieces, and 'Made in Sheffield' becoming as old-fashioned as a coach and horses, but with barely a whisper of public protest – and that in a city whose highly skilled workforce traditionally had job security and below-average unemployment. The frame both of the workaday and workless world seems here to be holding steady. Outside the town hall,

with not a tank or sentry in sight, the council lottery ('Win
£1,000 Today') is doing fair business from its kiosk, with
coloured bulbs hanging in the potted trees, and all as innocent
as a Christmas carol.

But Sheffield is no place for illusions, left or right; nor, as
the local economy goes under, for conventional battle-cries or
stout Yorkshire clichés. Indeed, nothing much can disguise
the prolonged dying of the steel and coal industries, on which
the whole region once depended; King Arthur of Barnsley has
no more chance of turning back the tide than King Canute – or
King Lud – had. Facing the plain truth, however, ought to be
easier here than in most places: Castle Square in Sheffield is a
'pedestrian underpass and subterranean shopping precinct,
with an ingenious roof of sky' in the guidebook, but it remains
'th'ole in t'road' to hard-bitten locals.

There have been no riots, says Blunkett – feeling for the
tea-level in his cup with his fingertips – partly because of
Sheffield council's 'sustained programme of physical regenera-
tion', partly because of what he calls Sheffield's 'community
ethos', and its 'almost unique affinity of feeling'. Others call it
an 'automatic Labour allegiance'; Charles Dodd, an old-timer
of seventy-three standing in a bleak wind outside the Duke
Street newsagent's, genially describes council policy as 'our
lads doing what they can with the money in the kitty'. And
with a lifetime in the AUEW behind him, he calls it a 'moral
duty' to 'go out and vote for them'. ('They're trying to take
away our rights in London. We ought to put up guards and
borders to stop it,' he jestingly added.) Certainly the despair
and hatred in the streets of Merseyside or the West Midlands,
the sense of trapped rage and imminent explosion, seem
absent here; and it is on this basis of 'collective feeling' that
Blunkett claims Labour's long-standing patrimony in Sheffield rests.

Other old-stagers, beached and boozing in the Labour Club
– where socialism and beer-swilling are synonyms – talk
comfortably of their 'heritage' and 'heirloom'. To Tom Mole,
a Rotherham bus conductor who went on to Ruskin as a

student, 'there's no real politics in it. Most of the people on the council, despite all the rhetoric, are not ideologically committed. It's more like the Mafia, or the Buffs and the Freemasons, a ladder to success. A donkey in a red rosette would get elected.' ('Not many donkeys have been,' said Blunkett.) For 'hissing Sid', Labour loyalties are 'all emotion'. Yet, in angular stride against local 'Marxism', even he had conceded that 'it's not just a surface sentiment, but deep feelings' – 'a working-class social feeling' he managed to call it; although, quickly stooping again in his judgment, added that 'subsidized council tenants know that it pays to vote Labour'. From the crowded cosiness of the Labour Club, even Ken Livingstone and the GLC appear like Johnny-come-latelies, political upstarts. To Tory Patnick, 'what's been going on in Sheffield' has been 'more insiduous than in London'; to Blunkett, whistling in the dark and with other visions, Sheffield has a 'different time-scale' and a 'longer-term view of social progress'.

'The difference between us and the GLC is that we're less radical, but more stable,' says Mike Bower (a 'key man' and a 'hard lad', according to Sid Cordle), six years on the city council, deputy chairman of its education committee, and an ex-NUJ northern organiser. Alex Waugh ('I'm not a trendy intellectual, I'm an ex-printer'), chairman of the Passenger Transport Executive which runs South Yorkshire's cheap buses – free on Sheffield's Inner City Circular, free for pensioners, and 2p anywhere for children – calls it 'permanent Labour control'. 'We can count on it,' says Bower.

You can even hear, as you go around, hard-edged Sheffield voices – sometimes off the record – on the subject of Livingstone's 'fancy' London 'tactics'. 'He wants to achieve what we have achieved,' says Roy Thwaites, the South Yorkshire county council's 'moderate' Labour leader and architect of the transport policy, 'but he hasn't got a clue. We built it all up slowly, from small beginnings. He should have held fire and come to us. I'd have said, "Hold fire, lad. Hold the line, and then move forward." ' But to the Tories in Sheffield and

South Yorkshire, inside and outside right alike, 'moving forward' is precisely the stealth of the 'creeping Marxism' which creates such paroxysms of terror.

To the outside left, into its second pint of bitter, it is equally precisely the 'reformism' which seeks 'to run the system better than the capitalists'. 'I'd get rid of the system,' said the Militant Mike Smith, clutching his *Guardian* and dreaming of the 'building of a mass revolutionary party'; 'cometh the crunch' – what crunch? – 'all that the reformists will try to do is to keep in power.' From the other flank, what Blunkett calls the replacement of a 'democracy of market forces' with a 'democracy of community decision-making' is, to Sid Cordle, the 'pursuit of an alien political philosophy' – 'they should come right out with it, and stand as communists' – which 'in a Christian sense' is 'positively evil'. Evil? 'They themselves may not be evil,' he says, closing his eyes, eyelids flickering, 'but they are trying by evil means to overthrow and destroy what exists by revolution.'

But what are the evil forces in Sheffield town hall, or London's County Hall, with their middle-class lives and large mortgages, actually doing? And how can what they are doing give rise to such opposed perceptions?

First, there is the refusal to 'hack the budget back to the government's targets', instead passing grant losses on to the public as rate increases. Sheffield's domestic rate, at £2·33 in the pound, is one of the highest in Britain; 'so high', says Patnick, shuffling through his papers, 'that you don't bother any more with the actual figure.' To the Tories, this is the 'spend, spend, spend, programme' which 'puts national policy in danger'. But to Sheffield Labour, on the other side of a widening political chasm, it means sustaining services and preventing job losses (that is, refusing redundancies) in what they call 'socially useful employment' – the 30,000 in part-time and full-time council jobs of one kind or another. But, second, it also means 'helping unemployed people and those on low incomes through the current depression', while taking the city deeper with each move and counter-move into a bitter regional planning and community battle with the centre. 'What Thatcherism is about', says Blunkett, 'is obvious here. We must instinctively go in the opposite direction.'

And as Whitehall applies the spending tourniquet, 'grant-related expenditure assessments', together with threatened further penalties and swingeing surcharges, are only the surface bureaucratic expression of a fear-stricken attempt to prevent the development of a local politics which is federal, even autonomist, in rhetoric and form, even if not (significantly) in substance; though to pretend that it is merely an issue of local domestic housekeeping, good, bad or indifferent, is itself falsely ingenuous. 'We're more determined, stubborn and ambitious than most authorities,' says Alex 'Transport' Waugh. 'We have come alive, under the pressure to abolish local government as we have known it,' says Blunkett.

Even buses and cheap bus fares are debated in South Yorkshire in the way other people wrestle over cruise missiles; as if life – the life of the community – depended on it. More than a quarter of a million have signed a Sheffield petition to 'save our buses'; 7,000 marched through the city. And if the left and right moralization of political issues has quickened nationally under radical Tory pressure, it has also produced a much lower threshold for triggering local outrage and political exaggeration; including when the actual shifts of direction being battled over are minimal. The South Yorkshire transport policy, says Mike Smith, is both a 'great sacred cow' and 'a tremendous step forward for working people'. At £65 million per annum in subsidy, the cost is 'outrageous' but it is the 'jewel in their crown', says Irvine Patnick. ('They've only collected £14 million a year in fares since the year blob,' he added.) 'The subsidy costs the average household a pint of beer a week,' says Waugh, translating economics into culture. 'It's all emotion,' Sid Cordle repeated, his fingers plaited together.

'Is freedom of movement socialism?' asked Roy Thwaites, mulling over and repeating the question I'd just put to him. 'Oh, yes it is, oh yes, lad,' he answered, in flat Yorkshire.

'Transport is a social service,' says Alex Waugh, 'and a key to the quality of life. With rising car ownership and all this tearing down of inner city areas for road construction, with increasing fares and skeleton services, we were getting down to the 20 per cent on the buses who can't drive a car, or could never afford one. But poor services for the poor are not on. Mobility at a reasonable price', he says flatly – the tone as intransigent as Thatcher's – 'is an individual right.' John Rawls seems to think so too, in his *Theory of Justice*; and so would John Stuart Mill, reincarnated.

In Sheffield, they talk about having 'kept their nerve' after Lord Denning's High Court excommunication of the GLC's cheap transport policy; about having broken the 'vicious circle' of rising fares, falling revenue, and further fare rises. Across the frontier, in Tory West Yorkshire, 'they've tried to cover their costs and lost a third of their passengers'. Here in South Yorkshire, Thwaites says, 'the unemployed can get out and about, out of the four walls, without worrying'. He calls it 'health-giving', 'therapeutic'. A 'real clever one', says Patnick, glumly. And local Labour is preparing to fight on the platforms and never surrender, when the Tories' new Transport Bill – which Patnick calls 'an answer to my prayers' and to his persistent lobbying of Mrs Thatcher – hits the city, with its new 'guidelines', new powers, and threats of surcharges and legal actions to stop what South Yorkshire is doing.

Yet it's not plain sailing, or driving, and there's a lot for this Tory counter-attack to build on, both local and national; and plenty of people in the working class to make a political Bailey-bridge, with their backs, for the Tories to charge across on. 'You know the kind of thing the Labour Party tells them,' says the man from the Pru, turning up the whites of his eyes in disconcerting fashion: ' "The Tories are going to take your buses away. Only the Labour Party can fight for the working classes." The trouble is five million trade unionists voted for us, not them, at the last election, and they will at the next one.'

Even Roy Thwaites unwittingly confirms that there are working-class morals and morals. 'The pensioners don't pay a

fare, and they think they're getting summat for nowt, some
do. Or the employees won't have any pride, or there'll be no
discipline, or everything'll go sloppy. "You what?" I tell 'em,
"we're not in the business of pride, we're in the business of
service." They say, "Wouldn't it be better for us just to pay a
bit?" That's back to the old self-respect nonsense, when
they've worked all their lives for it. So I say to 'em, "Get on a
bus and pay if you want to, love. You don't have to use your
pass. You can pay if you want, and no one'll stop you." '
An 'infiltration into the mind', Thwaites calls their 'respectable' scruples; and emerges, agitated, from his imaginary discourse.

Oh, there's real Labour canniness up here, never mind the
'left reformism'; and it is stronger than any theory. They can't
even put into words what it's made of themselves: 'reds and
Marxists' from one side, and 'Buffs and Freemasons' from
another, don't come within a mile of it. When they talk, in
private at least, about Ken Livingstone's 'stupid, bloody
tactics, that's what annoys us', you get a bit nearer to that
mixture   of   stubbornness,   labour-conservatism   (or
conservative-labourism) and careful cunning – 'know-how',
Alex Waugh calls it, but that's no use as a word either – which
would see off a revolution of any colour; opponents to 'right'
and 'left' of them have equal, and equally good, reason to
worry about getting past them.

Take council house sales. Some of Labour were for, some
against; they were bitterly divided over it. The Sheffield
'compromise', described with laughter, is to 'sell them very
slowly', not least by 'making sure that everyone knows it's not
all sweetness and light being a home-owner'. As a result, they
say, 'We've managed to get less applications to buy than
anywhere else.' Only 4 per cent of the 96,000 council tenants
in Sheffield want to buy their houses; 'we interview everybody
and we don't make it easy'. 'They put the pressure on,' says
Cordle, tautly. People are told, ' "If you buy, you may get a
problem family put next door to you." They get frightened
and withdraw their applications. It's absolute blackmail.' So

far, 800 council houses have been sold, 2,000 applications have been withdrawn, and three-quarters of the remaining applications are outstanding. 'It's not bad after three years,' says Blunkett, with grim satisfaction.

Indeed, he bloody-mindedly claims that 'it is Thatcher who has instigated what we are now about'. She, he says, 'needed to undermine local government, its confidence and ability, if she was going to be successful'. Instead, 'she has given us perspective and direction', and 'shown us that we will have to build on our community and collective feeling to make social progress'. Yet there is neither 'revolution' in the offing, nor, in a cold political climate, any working-class 'rank and file mobilization' in Sheffield; the outside-left, still clutching its *Guardian* (now rolled into a tube), claims that the inside-left couldn't achieve it even if it wanted. And there isn't any real collective enterprise, popular control or even much participation, whether in the GLC or Sheffield, all the ballyhoo notwithstanding. 'The man in the street can write or phone us,' says Alex Waugh, 'there is no populism or consumerism in South Yorkshire'; and no workers' control either.

'We were elected councillors as representatives of the public, through a democratic process,' Waugh adds briskly. 'If we're not doing our jobs, they can turn us out at the next election.' But, in fact, you'd think from listening to some of them, secure in office, that they were above politics altogether. 'Right and left don't really apply,' says Bower; 'the Labour movement here' is what he euphemistically describes as 'very well integrated'. 'Socialism in practice is common sense,' says Waugh, stiflingly. (Or is this the answer to Gramsci's prayer?) 'Something you can sell for the good of the whole community to anybody', he even calls it, and 'value for money'. 'The whole thing is a mixture,' says Blunkett, equally disconcertingly for those in search of a 'third way' through capitalism's thicket, 'of old and new, radical and middle of the road. It's important to hold the Labour group together.' Can such careful pilgrims really be the 'rabid Bennites and Marxists' of Cordle's Christian crusade and Patnick's Old Testa-

ment cursing? Or would the merest rustle in the political
undergrowth startle the Tory shire-horses?

The truth is, I think, that many of the protagonists
themselves – on the GLC too – don't know how to interpret
correctly what is going on. And wrangles about whether this is
some kind of utopian 'socialism in one county', or 'Marxism',
or the same old social democratic business organized by
'careerists' (who wouldn't recognize a grass-root if they saw
one), are insufficient. The trouble is, partly, that a combination of gas-and-water municipal socialism, Benthamite pater-
nalism, and Tammany trade unionism had it all stitched up
for so long in places like Sheffield – as they did in the Labour
Party nationally – that any departure, however embryonic,
from the dead Labourist status quo seems to threaten an
upheaval. So that Tory (and even Labour) cries of alarm in
local government signal the awakening of would-be town hall
federalists from this long coma, or 'yawn of boredom', as
Blunkett calls it.

It may amount to no more than a mulish exploration of the
limits of their statutory authority; but it is quite enough to
flutter the dovecotes when local Labour in Sheffield – and
elsewhere – covers its political nakedness with a few freshly
plucked fig-leaves. Thus, it is notions of 'democratic control
over the local economy', of the defence of community against
distant metropolis, and of the need to fashion new national
social policy initiatives 'from the bottom' ('if we had more
autonomy,' they say, 'we could contribute a great deal more to
national progress'), which have got the instinctive centralizers
in every party worried. To them, it is the proposition that
local government is 'central not peripheral' – 'we can show
them from here,' says Waugh, 'where they ought to be going' –
which is potentially explosive; not cheap fares as such, or
selling council houses slowly, and so forth.

For the meanings of such policy cut across traditional
demarcations between left, right and centre. Moreover, as an
anti-statist politics to win back 'greater local freedom' against
increasing Whitehall incursion, no wonder that it threatens the

vested Congress House and Westminster interests of Labour; while at the same time confusing the 'state-off-your-back' Tories, whose categories of political judgment are, in any case, usually confined to 'common sense' on the one hand, and 'Marxism' on the other. And who, on today's 'grass-roots left', can be bothered with Lenin's warning in 1907 that 'municipal socialism' – 'a specific trend to be found chiefly in England' – was 'reactionary' and 'particularly hopeless'? But why 'hopeless'? 'Because', Lenin answered, 'as long as it rules as a class, the bourgeoisie cannot allow any encroachment, even from the "municipal" point of view, upon the real foundation of its rule. Any attempt on the part of socialist municipalities to go a little beyond the boundaries of their normal, i.e. petty, activities . . . is invariably and absolutely vetoed in the most categorical fashion by the central government of the bourgeois state.'

Undaunted, David Blunkett's armoury of ideas – or ideals – is a well-stocked one, reaching far beyond a socialism-of-cheap-bus-fares. The need for the 'social ownership of local economic and industrial activity', and for 'local democratic control' over 'indigenous local skills and resources' has the Patnicks of the world reeling. 'While everybody else in the country is selling things off to private enterprise,' as the latter put it in the Grosvenor, 'this lot is taking them into public control. They even want to discriminate against firms making "socially undesirable products". If you're making atom bombs,' he said with incredulity, 'they won't welcome you in Sheffield, did you know that?' Veritably, a lost city, or Tory Sodom.

The reason why this means 'war' with Whitehall is that such a politics, however utopian, rests upon an uncomfortable premise: political power resides in the local control of resources, economic and social – the corollary itself of the painful discovery that the national crisis is destroying local economies, as it is destroying Sheffield's. Blunkett calls the 'new' political economy which flows from such awareness the 'democratic harnessing of the productive capacity of local industry' – 'skills, initiative, land, property, equipment' – 'to

the needs of the community'. To the Tories, this is simply a
'communist take-over'. But, so the town hall argument runs,
Sheffield council already buys £20 million worth of goods and
services a year from local firms, and directly employs 30,000
people; and in such 'Sheffield enterprises', the nucleus of a
'local socialist economy', *pace* Lenin, is allegedly already in
being. ('You can't wait for socialism until you have regenerated the economy,' says Blunkett, 'it has to begin here.') Local
Labour's next step would be to 'expand municipal trading
activities' – Blunkett mentions 'construction, components,
horticultural products' – and to 'develop trading relations with
other local authorities'. The council is even talking about
'import penetration' and 'import substitution', as if this were
the government of a Third World economy; which in a way it
now is, being so far north of Watford.

Sheffield's 'employment committee', set up in June 1981,
epitomizes what Friedmanite Toryism finds most redundant.
Advancing (though more in theory than in practice) upon
local industry with 'social strategy steering groups', 'action-
research projects', 'field-work teams', 'information banks' and
'inter-disciplinary cross-fertilization', the committee's im-
mediate purpose is to try to staunch the haemorrhage of job
losses – running at a rate of over 1,000 per annum in the city;
and perish the thought that there is no one, and nothing, that
could now staunch it. Its brief is also to 'impose a greater
degree of social planning upon the structural and technical
changes taking place in Sheffield'.

But all this 'polytechnic socialism' is a nightmare to the local
Tories; 'loony', Patnick calls it, shaking his bracelet. 'I
introduced myself to Mrs Thatcher at the last Tory Party
Conference. "Prime Minister," I said, "I'm Irvine Patnick,
Tory leader of the South Yorkshire county council." She
stood up and said to me, "Mr Patnick, you've got more
problems than I have." ' 'They're trying to bring money into
local industry all the time, pushing all the time,' complains Sid
Cordle, recoiling from the taint of any kind of public investment. 'It's very difficult to oppose, since on the face of it

they're trying to preserve jobs,' he admitted. 'But they're only doing it in ways they can get something out of. The idea of running the city as a really cost-effective enterprise is anathema to them. They employ political-social advisers on education, "strategy officers", and council house "persuaders",' he says, strenuously tolling them off on his fingers. 'In ten years, if they get away with all this' – 'new systems', Cordle calls them – 'they'll have made a fundamental change in the country.'

Yet, Blunkett and those who think like him in Sheffield are against 'blanket subsidies and public hand-outs'; 'they are a substitute' they tell you 'for a real social policy'. Blunkett himself is even opposed both to 'bureaucratic public corporations' and to 'social democratic welfarism'. It's not only Tories, in the face of this, who may lose their ideological bearings. 'We have to change the existing perception of community provision,' he says, the black Labrador lying at his feet, unmoving. 'But it will be a hell of a struggle to get away from it, while people see themselves as clients of a paternalistic welfare system. It's a problem of the tragically low level of political literacy in this country, the lowest in the industrial world. And we have to change from a consumerism of individual self-interest to a democracy of community decision-making; we've got to throw our weight behind people, especially people with ideas for co-operative forms of enterprise, and work with them, not for them. But changing the structure is not enough. It's a question of education.'

The reach and pungency of the hostility *inside* the Labour movement to this sort of politics cannot be underestimated. Indeed, the very same people who are 'Marxist pseudo-intellectuals now abounding in local government' to Patnick on the outside-right, are 'petit-bourgeois intellectuals with paper qualifications' to Mike Smith on the outside-left, and 'trendy academics' or 'the increasing lecturer-type' to the AUEW stalwart, or centre-half, who leads Labour on the county council. 'The youngsters from the polys who want the revolution tomorrow, all guns blazing', is Roy Thwaites talking. 'They can't teach us our jobs, thank you very much. If they want an Oxford debating society,' he says, flattening his vowels further, 'they can get in a corner. What they can't do, and we can, is talk logic, common-sense logic. We're not in utopia. We're not daft enough to go into fancy theories.'

'I preferred the old trade union socialists who had their fingers on the pulse,' says the Tory; 'no amount of nice fancy Marxist talk will get the bloke on the dole a job,' says Labour. They could be the same man, with the same vowel sounds and the same meaning; 'when have they ever done an honest day's work?' is the unspoken next comment from both of them. 'They want the edges knocking off them,' says Thwaites, who also has a thing or two about 'Trots and nutters'. 'It's the working class's own representatives who will throttle hissing Sid as well as the academics in the Labour Party,' says the Militant supporter. Blunkett himself speaks well on the subject of such 'working-class chauvinism', which he describes as a matter of 'who can drink the most – when you get down to it – or whether you were born in an orange-box. I was born in a council house myself, and I'm proud of it. But I don't think you should have to play the working-class card, or wear it on your sleeve. The more secure you are,' he adds, 'the less you have to do it.'

But 'workerism' is only one kind of political reaction in Sheffield. 'As soon as the HMS *Sheffield* went down,' says the Reverend Alan Billings, Labour's deputy leader (who, in dog collar, calls his colleagues 'comrades'), 'you couldn't talk about the Falklands. You'd have had your house smashed up, or your throat cut.' And if you scratch the surface, you'll find some of the old guard, Tory and Labour, in the city – and far beyond – alike nostalgic for the old days, when Labour was the cloth cap which knew its station, and Tory was a lot more blue blood and a bit better manners. It was obviously all too much for the previous Labour leader of the city council, George Wilson, who has joined the SDP ('a more common-sense approach,' said Cordle). When the familiar ideological landmarks, like the old terraces, get grubbed up for redevelopment, some folk don't know where they are going.

To Blunkett, the issues are quite different. 'Thatcher has been stimulating attitudes which lead logically to fascism. City democracy – which is as relevant today as in Greece 2,500 years ago – and a healthy community politics, are a bulwark against it.' 'I talk to journalists,' declares Patnick, gathering up his untidy papers (including ragged clippings from the *Morning Star*) in the Grosvenor, 'and say, "This is what is happening in Sheffield. These are not socialists, these are full-time Marxists, running the council for their own benefit. Don't, for God's sake, let it happen in your area." The only way out for me is death,' he says, offering me his junk apocalypse, 'or running. And I'm not running.'

Over in the town hall, 'Another dose of adrenalin in their bloodstreams,' says Blunkett, of Thatcherite Whitehall, 'and they'd endeavour to wipe us out entirely.' It's all *patria o muerte*, this game of municipal Snakes and Ladders; or, a 'revolution by stealth' (led by one man and his dog) in England's fourth largest and very cautious city. 'Ours', says Roy Thwaites, his confidence suddenly ebbing, 'is the model the others are following.' 'We've become the laughing-stock of the whole country,' said Patnick. The 'front line', the man from the Pru called it, twisting his fingers.

'I'm Getting Out Before It Fall On Me'

May 1983
This is Slade Road, Erdington, in the leaden shadow of
Birmingham's Spaghetti Junction, a cat's cradle of damp-
stained concrete. Through the venetian blind and double
glazing, from an upstairs window, you can see Enoch's
nightmare black figures plodding its pavements, emerging
from its terrace shops, shambling homewards; or what passes
for home in this breaker's yard of twenty-five years of
immigrant hope and effort.

The glass ashtray on the window-sill bears a portrait of Sir
Alexander Bustamante; on the sideboard is Michael Manley,
behind glass, and the *West Indian Digest* lies on the red plush
sofa. There are coloured grasses in a vase, a discreetly framed
Scottish ptarmigan stalking the careful decoration around the
fireplace, and a four-foot-long beachscape, with foaming
grey-blue breakers, in photographic blow-up. 'Britain for the
Brits,' Hyacinth Wilson has just said, drily. (Forty-three per
cent – a huge 113,000 – of Birmingham's inner city are
'ethnics'.) 'They are welcome to it.'

These are bitter days, growing more bitter, of black cir-
cumstance dire beyond correction, in a Brummie whirlpool of
too high infant mortality and illegitimacy rates, large numbers
of pensioner-only and lone parent households, high crime
rates and levels of overcrowding, extensive areas of vacant and
derelict land (and of heavy metal pollution), low levels of car
ownership and inadequate 'public open space' for recreation.
'You are looking at a person', she says, 'who doesn't really care
any longer.' She cares greatly; 'it is dreadful to feel powerless,'
she was to say later. Hyacinth Wilson, who came to Britain
from Jamaica twenty-two years ago, at the age of nineteen, is
one of Birmingham's nine qualified black social workers – out
of a total of over 370 – and deep in the gradually rising tide, at
All Saints' Hospital, of black mental illness.

An ex-Ruskin student, on her bookshelves are Robert Tressell and Harold Robbins, the *New English Bible*, Marilyn French and Steve Biko; together with Virtue's *Home Tutor*, *The Death of White Sociology* and Macaulay's *History of England*, bound in leatherette, in four volumes: markers in a long journey of aspiration from Jamaica, now nosediving into the dump which has been made of the Midlands by urban decline and industrial closure. Over 40 per cent of Birmingham's manufacturing jobs have gone in the last ten years; and 31·8 per cent are now jobless in the 'core' inner city – its population down by 20 per cent in a decade – of whom 38 per cent are 'ethnics', with West Indians the largest group among them.

Beside the electric-blue beachscape, with Joe Nez and his Top Six singing on the record-player and a red telephone on a glass-topped side-table, she speaks of her 'disappointment, anger and frustration'; of the 'lack of facilities, lack of knowledge, lack of willingness to change and lack of respect for other cultures' which she encounters in her work. ('I have a lot to protest about in this shitty system,' she added, 'please don't protect me.') According to her, about a quarter of the patients in the All Saints' acute wards – referred by GPs, relations and social workers – are young West Indians; many of them 'Rastas, or pseudo-Rastas, or whatever you want to call them'. (There are apparently very few, if any, young Asians.) 'Schizophrenia' and 'depression' are the main diagnoses; or the 'usual labels'.

'Everyone knows there is a special problem with black psychiatric patients, but no one knows what the answer is. Now,' she says, 'they've got a new name for all the aggressive and depressive symptoms: "*ganja* psychosis", they call it. What they say is that these patients were probably psychotic to start with, but because they smoke *ganja*, the psychotic episodes are accelerated. There may be something in it. I'd start beyond that. I'd look at the reasons why they began to smoke *ganja*, and why it affects black people this way in Britain, and not in Jamaica. The trouble is that they don't

realize the problem is not marijuana.' Instead 'it's twenty years
deep,' she says, 'in poor housing, in lack of nursery vacancies
for blacks' – 'white nurseries' is her term for it – 'in being
dragged from one child-minder to another. The onset of the
psychotic symptoms has a lot to do with years of experience of
racism. It's endemic in the education system, in all the
institutions. Twenty years on, these are the kids on the streets,
in the wards and in the prisons. But they're only a small part of
a lost generation.' Lost? 'Yes,' she says flatly, 'lost. And
they're bringing up another generation to live like they live,
and to think like they are thinking. That's the generation
Britain is going to have to reckon with.' ('There are some of
them so radical,' as she put it, 'I couldn't introduce you.')
'Nothing Britain can do is going to change the bitterness and
hate of this generation. They're handing that down beautifully
to their children,' she says, wide-eyed, as if horror-struck
herself at what she is saying.

On a shelf, she has four fluffy toy animals in small
transparent boxes, gift-packed and silk-ribboned, and her
son's West Bromwich Albion bric-à-brac and insignia. She
comes back to the condition of her patients. 'Then, they get
put on section twenty-six. It means that they can be treated
compulsorily under the Mental Health Act.' ('If you don't
agree,' she says, eyes flashing, 'they'll bring in another social
worker.') 'They're trapped from then on', she adds, wincing,
'in a cycle of "sectioning" and aggression. I'm not saying that
there aren't real mental problems. I'm not disputing that black
people suffer from mental disorder. But the whole thing is
getting worse as economic circumstances worsen, and resources get scarcer and scarcer. It's the constant aggression. In
England, if you act like that, you're "mad". It's mistaken for
mental disturbance. "He must be paranoid," they say, "look at
the way he's struggling." And when they really kick up, they'll
get locked away in a secure unit under section sixty.' In the
shining grey-tiled hearth is a brown pot shire-horse and cart.
'But the simple truth is that no real attempt has been made to
understand emotions, no real caring, no attempt to get at the

real reasons for the aggression. A person must match the system every time. It's never the other way around. You don't have to go to Russia to see rebellion diagnosed as madness.'

Outside, it is sleeting cats and dogs; one day it may rain fire and brimstone. 'You won't find the answer in any textbook,' she says (I wasn't trying to); 'and going back twenty years of these kids' lives is no use either.' It was, a moment ago. Now it sounds like another albatross to hang around the neck of a declining nation. 'The British spent 400 years beating our language and culture out of us, remember? That's what slavery was about. It was a punishable offence to speak your own language,' she says fiercely. 'And that's what is at the root of all the aggression. Nothing the British can do now is going to change it.' The roaring in my ears is more than a match for Spaghetti Junction; or those grey-blue breakers.

There is already a new generation of young black derelicts, many abandoned by their parents who 'would see it as, "I've worked twenty years in the factories, I've tolerated all the shit in this country to look after you, and instead of getting on in school you've joined the no-good Rastas." When the parents are really desperate, going back home – getting out, and leaving them to it – is seen as the only answer. Often you find they don't recognize them as their children any more; and their relations who are still here don't want to know them.' These, or some of these, are the 'wanderers' in broken-down Birmingham lodgings, discharged from mental hospitals, or borstals, or prisons; and around the hospital dustbins you'll see, she says, jobless and homeless black scavengers looking for food scraps.

'So many of them' have been what she calls 'hammered' – with histories of being 'arrested for no good reason, taken to police lock-ups, brought to court, remanded to Winson Green or sent to Warwick Central or Risley, made to wait trial for a year or longer and then found not guilty when no evidence is offered, or transferred under section sixty' – 'that they're in a state of total withdrawal'. As for discharged black mental patients, 'most live in lodgings and hostels. But they can't stay in all day, and since they have no jobs, they have nowhere to go. Many of them spend their chitties' – social security bills of credit for rented accommodation – 'on *ganja*. They can't manage money, can never pay their heating or electricity bills, and end up in the bookies, a lot of them. A black man', she says – flurries of sleet at the window – 'doesn't want to use a paintbrush in an occupational therapy centre' ('you can't tell him to paint'), 'so he wanders the streets and hangs around the hospitals. At least there the staff is friendly to them, will offer them food and let them sit around, or do jobs in the kitchen. At night, they go back to their lodgings.'

From what she says, neither the dole (nor Soul), nor psychiatric social work – nor the big stick of the racist – will ever get within miles of this mess now; and you can stuff Labour's 'alternative programme'. 'White people', she claims, 'don't understand the needs of these people. What's more [changing her tack] they should not be expected to understand them. If they were given a million pounds each, ten million, it wouldn't make any difference.' And, among the older West Indians especially, she claims there is 'a mental exodus going on from Britain, even with those who are not actually leaving'. What does she mean? 'I mean, even more would like to go than are going, but they have no savings. Many have lost contact. Others are ashamed of going back like tramps, with the same suitcases they left with. How do you go back, and say you've been in the "mother country" twenty years? How do you face them?'

On the record-player, a black voice is moodily singing, 'Have you ever been outside when the rain is falling, In the rain, in the cold, in the stormy night?' 'It's Britain for the Brits,' she says again. 'But I'm not complaining. They fought for it, stole for it, killed for it.' ('The only buggers who don't know that', she added, 'are the working class.') 'It's theirs, every inch of it. They deserve it.' But it's enough to make you blench, this kind of darkness; or blackness.

Further up the Slade Road, at the Spade, Hammer and Pen – a black club 'for the labouring class, the technician and the intellectual of all races, creed and tongue', with a sub of fifty pence per month, a small council grant and about 100 members – furrowed black brows are gathered around the formica-topped tables. Here, the respectable despairs of the middle-aged, many deep into unemployment, and dismayed by their 'wasted' decades in Britain, congregate in a near-dumb silence.

A mechanic when he was in Jamaica, Colvin Marshall ('I'm a working man'), twenty-three years in England, ex-Rover Solihull, seven years and still working on the wet-deck in a BL paintshop – 'the work's hard, the track is always going on, all day long' – says, shoulders hunched, that 'in those days you came here, but what you tried to achieve you didn't get'. ('No,' say the others, *sotto voce* and sombre.) 'I've always been working, but I'm struggling to pay my bills. Some years ago, I had a chance to go to Canada. Now, every day my wife get at me and say, "You turned it down." Now there is nothing for the kids, nothing. They can be brainy, go to Eton [grimacing], but there's still no future. When I get on a bus, and they see you coming from work, they give you dirty looks. You feel it. When pressure meets the local people this is the crisis you face, a whole lot of insults.' ('The native of this country', as he puts it, 'resents it when you have a job, and they haven't.') 'We as blacks stand out in this unemployment.'

Joe Lee, ex-Alcan, ex-guard at Birmingham's New Street station, and seven years working the trains out to Stratford-on-Avon, is unemployed (but working *sub rosa* as a garage mechanic); sunk in a dark-brown study and natty brown suit, in broad pin-stripe. He says, 'Everything getting tense and dead. I can't just pick up a job nowhere.' (He calls it 'a crisis which seems to follow you', and describes his dole money as 'not good enough'.) 'At the labour exchange, either everything you touch is poison, or a warder at Winson Green prison.' ('They have so many racists to deal with the public,' says Colvin, 'social security, tax office. They're against you, the way they treat you. Most of them on the counter are racists, what chance do you stand?')

Joe came to Britain for 'five years' more than twenty years ago, wanting to go to a college of further education. 'When I came, I thought I'd be in a certain position. I wasn't looking for this fluctuating situation.' What did you expect? 'The teaching at home', he continues, 'misled us. We heard all about the kind-hearted white man. Everything is nice and bright, mother country. I found it in the opposite direction. This is my bitterness.' He is heard in silence; you can hear the gas-jets hissing. In the last four years unemployment among Birmingham West Indians has risen threefold. 'It's a long execution,' Joe says. He has fat hands and ringed fingers. 'The black man', says Clifford Wilson, ex-BL and now on the dole, 'done suffer more pain in this country than any other nation'; rapping turning briefly into lyrics, as I shrink into my raincoat. He is spruce in his nylon-fur-lined jacket. 'They come to you and say "no colour bar". They give you sweet mouth and throw you down there.' 'You can easily get down when you get propelled,' Joe says. These are mild and decent men; hurt, depressed and anxious.

In this sort of company, I have already discovered that you cannot mention the trade unions. 'They are all white,' says Colvin; 'we have one black convener.' 'They don't want to know about us,' says Joe, who was sacked on the spot by British Rail for 'late de-training', followed by a stiff letter from the station-master, and has been 'hard-pressed' since. 'I think the trade unions should be scrapped,' he declares intemperately, 'I detest them.' This is working-class anti-unionism with a difference: the bitterness of black labour, with grievances unregarded. I heard it right across black Birmingham, with few exceptions. Hyacinth Wilson, ex-Ruskin and all, even said that 'the trade unions and the Labour Party are the worst enemies of black people, the worst. At least you know where you stand with Tories. You know they hate you.' Head in hands, you might well ask, 'What's wrong with this country?' 'Nothing,' replies Clifford Wilson. 'The world has never been bad. It's the people.'

He has been out of work since October last, after seventeen

years of sweat in the BL foundry at Longbridge, and twenty-two years in this country 'August coming' – 'just earning to keep the family'. 'The white boys got the piecework,' he adds with resignation. 'They don't give you the same slice they are eating.' 'That's what we all face now,' says Colvin, 'the chances are nil.' What did the blacks get? 'We would be down on the brush, sweeping, sweeping,' says Wilson. He looks down at his hands, turning them from side to side. 'I'm not a trained man. I saw no progress.' The others, knowing it all, don't even glance at him. 'If I'd got my own house, I'd be ninety-five per cent better. It's always the poor man who be suffer most.' There is a long silence. 'I didn't come to walk the streets.'

No one stirs; 'I'm sorry that I came to this country,' he says, looking down at his feet. 'Seventy per cent of us', says Joe, 'were deluded.' 'Most people have regrets,' declares Hubert Tulloch, a club founder-member who qualified as a chiropodist at forty, after running a taxi business with a cousin and then working in the GPO's supply section. He also had a job with the Co-op which 'lasted three hours', after his first encounter with the 'gaffer'. 'I didn't like how him talk, so I just walked out. These days, no one can walk out,' says Hubert. Now he has a small terrace-end barber's shop, almost beneath Spaghetti Junction. Most people have regrets? 'Yes.' What do you mean? 'Let down in various ways, disappointed with the government and the British people,' he answers. ('I don't think our MP would let you down,' demurs Colvin; 'he does,' Joe Lee says.) 'They brought us here in the first place. We were far ahead of the Indians. We could have been better looked after.'

Hubert has a round, smiling face, balding and avuncular; a Labour Party ward activist, married to a white woman, and in England donkey's years. He is well known in the area, respected by black and white alike. 'I didn't need to come, exactly,' he says. 'I had a job in Jamaica with the B. & J. B. Tobacco Company. But I thought it would be a good opportunity to do something. I've been happy here, I have no regrets at all. But you see people who struggled all their lives, but never achieved what they expected. They're fed up. Some people have lands back home, but they're only going because they're fed up here. They feel they could make it better where they belongs. But, sometimes, I think we ourselves self-contributed to our downfall.' ('I don't agree,' says Colvin.) Hubert's past tenses have their own resonance, as if pointing homewards. 'The Pakistanis and Indians', he goes on, 'have driven us into the back seat.' He is listened to with respect; an elder. Voices, in assenting chorus for the first time, say, 'It is, it is.'

Colvin alone disagrees with the defeatism. 'Not everyone', he says, 'is going to sit back and put up with their situation. Maybe the older. But the young won't stand for it.' Joe Lee says, 'We get nowhere, we doesn't believe ourselves and see it through. I've seen it in the factory.' ('Yes,' say the voices together.) 'The Indians are more patient. They have more duty. They will put up with anything.' ('I support you there,' says Clifford Wilson.) 'They grasped the jobs. It was only the browns they could get to do them. I've seen the gaffers kick something to them, and tell them to pick it up. The West Indians'd kick it back.' (Laughter.) 'They'd put up with things more than you,' says Clifford; 'less social life,' adds Colvin. 'They have their feet down now,' says Joe, gloomy. In fact, what seems to have happened is that since their arrival in the 1950s, instead of being 'upwardly mobile', West Indians – unlike Asians – have largely remained at the base of the labour market, where they started. Now, with unemployment, they are drifting out of it altogether.

There is a sickly pallor in the neon strip-lighting. 'Are you thinking of leaving?' I ask Joe. He has brown suede shoes and a tiny pistol tie-pin. 'Yes,' he says, 'the pressure seems to be on. But many of the ladies and kids are not ready to go. You're finding a barrier in your homes. But any sensitive person who can make it home should be going.' However, most have not got the passage money, feel that they have given their lives to this country, and before they go should be recompensed for their service. Nor is any real economic improvement expected under Labour. In these dark times and places, there are no illusions.

'When she applies the pressure, we'll have to go,' says Joe. She? 'Mrs Thatcher.' (Even Hubert, phlegmatic, murmurs that 'the day will come when we have to flee'.) Are you joking? He ignores the question. 'It's in the back of many people's minds to leave as soon as they can,' says Hubert; 'it's no joke here, things are getting really serious.' How many people? 'Sixty per cent,' says Hubert, 'if the government said, "Here's a good handshake." ' 'Seventy-five per cent,' say the others, again in chorus. Some, especially of the older folk, they all say, have already sold out and gone – to Canada, to the United States, back to the West Indies. More are waiting ('oh yes, definitely') or hoping, or saving, for departure, Hubert Tulloch included.

'Places for West Indians are always near police stations or prisons,' says George Adamson. He seems cautious, a quiet-spoken Barbadian in a cap, muffler and anorak, twenty-eight years in England and vice-president of the West Indian Federation Association, a community organization which started life as an ex-servicemen's centre. Its premises are the old mission across the road from Winson Green prison. At night, with its crenellated towers and battlements under fierce illumination, the gaol looks like a Disneyland castle set in a rotting sodium-lit landscape that would make an angel weep with anger. As much as half of the pre-1919 housing stock round here – and there is a lot of it – is classed as 'unfit for habitation'. Against the mission wall, in the rain flurries, a foundered van is mouldering up to its axles in the mud ruts; an old side-road, cobbled, ends in a boarded-up wasteland of rubble.

Upstairs in the office – with its fitted floral carpet and a reproduction of Velazquez's Rokeby Venus over the mantel-shelf – Adamson, carefully lighting a cigarette, says, 'We came to England around the 1950s, getting away from low wages and unemployment in the West Indies, hoping to follow up a skill, do five years. Ninety-five per cent never saw themselves here long term. We're like plants which belong to the tropics. We came to return.' He is sitting sidelong in profile, muffled under his cap. 'First, you figured you'd save,' he says, exhaling. 'Then, you sent for a girl, you moved from a room to a flat, and then to a house. You settled down. Society is so geared that you're hooked.' He was a 'works accountant' for ten years – with a strong sense of taxes paid over the years by West Indians, and 'not much to show for it' – and for the last five has sold insurance.

Michael Blake, sitting beside him, is a voluntary youth worker at the centre, a welder unemployed since September 1982. He is a small quick man in a black felt stovepipe hat – someone calls it a 'three-pint' – with a spade beard and gold neck-chain. There is something blazing in his eye, making him seem like a Mayflower Puritan, or a black Guy Fawkes on a short fuse. 'If they'd known what they'd meet,' he says, his voice hard-edged, 'they'd never have come in the first place.' What did they meet? He seems to ignore the question and the questioner. 'The kind of work we had to do. Never being recognized for it. Whites moving out as if we had the plague. Places becoming overcrowded with our people. And the same whites', he says with scorn, or worse, 'who ran away thirty years ago when we moved in, have moved right back in there', as slum rehabilitation (and rising rents) squeeze many of the blacks deeper into their ghettos. It is a swift and bitter review, rooted in anger; a vista of another cobbled dead-end paved with good intentions.

Around the Calor gas-fire they talk about themselves as victims, like a conclave of synagogue elders. In their age-group, men in their mid-forties, there has been a high local rate of increase – itself accelerating – in unemployment. Adamson thinks, phlegmatically, that 'there'll always be scapegoats'. Hilton Alleyne, a Barbadian in a neat suede jacket, his shoes highly polished, says, 'We stopped coming in '72, but still they say we're coming.' 'The white man getting no work,' says Blake, 'the Indian ain't got it, the black ain't got it.' 'They can see me with a bag of potatoes,' complains Alleyne obliquely, 'and say, "How's he managing it? How's he doing that?" ' 'The foundries are gone now,' says Blake sharply, 'they can't say it.' 'The whole vicinity is on the dole,' adds Alleyne, 'so who can say the blacks are taking it?'

The eye strays to the Venus's framed backside and her young winged attendant over the mantelpiece, buttocks as white as snow in a dark setting. 'When my old man and old lady came here,' says Blake, 'they went into diminishing industries', such as foundry work and what he calls 'minimal tasks'; while 'the natives' – 'so to speak,' he adds wrily – 'were advancing in better fields and skills'.

There is a difficult silence. 'In those days,' says Adamson, inhaling, 'you had to break through a lot of barriers. On the buses they said, "Your thinking is too slow to be a driver" [eyes closed, laughing].. You couldn't be a bus inspector, you couldn't sell insurance. Then, you had no choice.' 'My kids have got a choice,' says Blake hotly. 'They're saying, "Now, we want it equal." They're not taking anything that's thrown at them.' 'My daughter has no job,' says Alleyne, hands folded in his lap, a sharp crease in his trousers. 'They write back and say she's too intelligent for what they're wanting.' 'It used to be the other way,' Adamson comments, 'you were not qualified enough', the others nodding, their brief laughter at such conundrums uneasy. 'The older folks ain't going to get anything now,' says Blake. 'A lot of guys with over twenty years have decided to pull up,' says Adamson. 'The majority of us are trapped,' says Alleyne.

They speak of returning home, the focus – it seems – of most West Indian thought, and quick to surface. 'There's not one in a million who wants his bones to be buried in this country,' Adamson says. 'With kids and debts, there is no way you can save to go home,' says Blake, his voice astringent. 'How can the older children help you, when there's no jobs and no wages?' Adamson, dragging on his cigarette between pinched fingers, says that 'some old West Indians won't leave their children'; and Alleyne that 'even if parents want to go,

the kids don't want to'. 'The outlook is getting so bleak,'
Adamson says, as calm as ever, tapping another cigarette out
of his packet, 'a lot of the kids are getting interested'
in leaving. 'They don't see themselves getting the breaks,
they don't join the police, that kind of thing, they
don't see themselves as part of Britain. In America, the
blacks see themselves as black Americans. In England
not many see themselves as black British.' He is on thin
ice, and Blake's voice cuts through him: 'In America, the
blacks used to call themselves niggers. They didn't know
where they came from. In England, we know. We're from
the West Indies.' He himself is planning to leave, or so he
says, but is fierce about his children.

'I don't want them to follow me,' he declares, his voice
rising, the veins, in the room's heat, standing out in his
forehead. 'I say to them, "You have a choice now. This is your
country." At school, on the playground, they tell my daughter, thirteen, "Why don't you pack up and go home, blackie?"
Next minute', he says, explosive, 'you have this careers'
master guy career-talking to her. Career-talking! I say to her,
"You learn, until you can learn no more. You learn to go to
university and be a lawyer, because we're going to need
lawyers for the fighting we'll have to be doing. And you don't
ever forget, you were born in Moseley, Birmingham 13," ' he
says, his voice high and eye burning; ' "and you're going to
live right here" ' – sitting, legs crossed, and stubbing his knee
with his thumb – ' "and you're going to die right here, in
England." '

There is a rage in this – 'they'll burn and loot, they'll
become like another Alabama,' says Adamson quietly – which
only goodwill, unrequited, keeps in check. 'People are talking
more openly than they did. Ten years ago they had jobs. Now
they've got nothing to lose.' He remains impassive. 'Plenty of
West Indian parents talk to their children like Blake,' adds
Alleyne, coolly.

'Everybody knows someone going. Two families I know
went back last week,' continues Adamson, gazing into the

middle distance, his back to the prison; 'when you've been out of a job two years, your whole thinking is different.' There is a silence: 'quite a few going back, drifting away,' muses Alleyne. 'They left the West Indies to go back better,' says Blake, tying his own Gordian knot tighter; 'rather than going back the same way they were, with one suitcase like they came, they'd prefer to die here.'

It would take a black Houdini to escape these dilemmas: of joblessness, of time passing, of their own kids born in Britain but without a future, and of the shame of the prodigal's return, empty-handed. 'Some are going with their redundancy payment, rather than just swallow it,' says Adamson, 'with them same old suitcases, but filled with a few five-pound notes of their money.' 'Some may not have a home to go to,' says Blake. 'The kids are here' – in Birmingham 13, for example – 'so who are they going back to?' 'There is no way out of it,' says Alleyne, 'only pack up, and go.' They are like the children of Israel, stranded in the wilderness of the West Midlands, with only Enoch Powell as a prophet. 'If all the old people' – people who've 'done twenty years here, going to feel the cold till the day they die, and only a few pounds to live off' – 'say "Let's go home",' Blake declares (meeting himself coming backwards), 'and the kids are left to face the pressure, they'll burn from here to Buckingham Palace.'

'You see the way they're walking in the streets,' says Alleyne, 'an explosion with youth is coming.' Adamson, perspiring, gets up to turn the gas-fire lower. 'We ought not to be talking about going home,' says Blake, who has just been talking about it. 'We've got to be powerful here, like the Jews or the Italians.' (The Italians?) 'We need special funds earmarked for blacks' – 'give us the money and let us do things for ourselves' – 'not money for repatriation. I'm not going to live through this recession, and then go home with ten thousand pounds and lie down under a banana tree.' He could do worse. 'If you give me forty thousand,' he continues, wheeling and dealing, 'I'd think about it. But I've put too much into this to run away from it. If things improve, I want to share it. Me's English, and no one's going to stop me coming back through Heathrow.'

The room stirs fitfully. Even the Venus, stretched out on her blue-black draperies, seems to shift her position. 'There'll always be talk of repatriation, but the only time it will come to fruit is if we do nothing. If the blacks sit on their arses, and don't become more politically active, involved in the economic life in this country,' Blake says passionately, 'if we remain here as a negative force, there'll be a catastrophe.' Active through the trade unions, for example? 'The trade unions?!!' The room dissolves in laughter. 'Oh man!' says Blake, 'they were as bad as Enoch Powell. They're crap, a waste of space.' 'Blacks were just subscribers,' says Adamson, in a voice which sounds tired of the whole subject. 'With us, the management and the unions were like that,' Blake says, plaiting his dark index fingers together. 'They never wanted black people to get a lot of money. They never took an interest when it's black people losing their jobs. Man, we were just adding to the funds. Those trade unions couldn't help no black members,' he adds, 'the way they look at humans.' 'We've seen it all on the shop-floor,' says Adamson; 'you're down to the grindstone with the working class.' It seems a terminal subject, mostly seen in the past historic, and as if beyond redemption.

At 10 p.m. on a Friday night in Soho Road, Handsworth – an area where there is over 50 per cent youth unemployment – clapped-out Cortinas full of black dudes, dressed to kill and with fathomless eyes, are cruising, or parked in the club forecourts. A sign on the door of the Faith and Confidence says 'No woollen hats allowed'. Inside, a few loose-limbed young bucks in woollen hats are playing pool, two doubled-up girls (arses in tight silk) giggling in the passage, and a funky singer mooning to the near-empty room, like a man whistling in darkness. The nude calendar above the bar is of a white woman. In the cluttered back-office Bernard Francis, the secretary, says there are 300 members – 'mostly older people' – and that the numbers are falling.

A Jamaican twenty years in England, and a welding en-

gineer by trade ('electricity and gas council approved'), he has
had his own side-line, since the late 1960s, organizing holiday
charters to the West Indies, and as a shipping sub-agent.
There's always been, he says, 'a trickle of people who've had
enough', going home. In the mid-1970s it started to be the
'in-thing' to 'go back for a year and test the ground', or 'do the
groundwork'. But 'over the past twelve months they're going
home full-stop, and that's it'. According to him, it's the old
ones who are going, and leaving their children – 'disrupting
the community', even – 'downright fed up with the economic
situation, plus the way people live in this country'. ('And
there's no way you can come back and start again at fifty.')
They are people 'whose hopes did not mature' – made
redundant with no hope of further employment, or going, not
because of the recession, but 'because they're ready to go, the
time has come. When a man is ready he'll go, there's nothing
which will hold him, even if he's got nothing in Jamaica.'

'Ninety-five per cent of the Jamaicans', Francis adds (offering yet another percentage), 'came to make money and then go
home. But what happened? He came here, he gets a wage and
thinks he'll save. But it's all against him, winter coats,
paraffin, gas-bills. The weather hits you. He can work for
twenty years, but the system is that what he gets goes right
back into the system. All he's got is a council house. He says
he's going home, he's had enough.' ('Even the younger ones
are beginning to think Jamaica. They're saying, "We can go to
work beautifully down there, own a car." They're thinking,
"What the hell are we doing here in England?" ')

And, now, with three or four (or, occasionally, more)
thousand pounds of redundancy money in their pockets –
'enough to buy themselves a little truck to sell fish' – 'they are
telling themselves', he continues, 'that they're not going to get
any better here, so they might as well go, instead of staying
and eating it all up. They're not going to bury themselves in a
situation where they'll never get out at all.' Others are ready to
leave, but waiting to be made redundant; 'if it wasn't for the
depression,' he adds, 'they'd never have picked up that kind of

money, no way. What happened to most of us', he goes on, in a rush of candour, 'is that after the first year, we went round looking for girls, married, started to get kids, and forgot about what we came here for in the first place. You buy a house, buy furniture, spend everything and that's where the decline starts. The longer you stop, the worse it becomes.' Once back, he claims that the returnees, after 'twelve months having a hard time, getting back in the groove' – or 'finding problems in Jamaica' – are what he calls 'quite jolly'. ('Go back to England? What for?') What about unemployment in Jamaica? 'We never see anyone working there anyway,' he says, laughing like the girls in the passage. 'When I hear about unemployment there, I think, "What are you talking about?" They do their own thing in Jamaica.' In the distance, you can hear an answering laughter.

His own parents – 'my mum was a punch-press operator, my dad was in the post office' – have already gone. 'They came to me one morning and said, "We're going home, we've had enough." I said to my dad, "Why don't you wait for your pension?" He said, "I don't want it." So I said, "Take the settee, take the furniture with you." ' Are they happy? 'Oh, Christ, quite well off, quite happy,' he replies, conviction paling on the instant. Are they? 'Back home, they're the envy of the village.' Yet 13 per cent of the inmates of Kingston's Bethlehem mental hospital are said to be returnees, stigmatized by failure. 'When they get home,' Francis himself says, 'people say you've been sent out of England, Margaret Thatcher running you out, or England drive you mad. Nowadays, if you go back, you're not a successful person, not someone who's made it.'

Would he himself go? 'I'd go, oh yes.' There is silence. You can hear the click of billiard balls, and a forlorn, distant singing. 'I know what you're going to ask me,' he says. Oh? 'How much will I be taking out, is what you were going to ask me.' I don't like the question, say I. 'And I', he says, in black ankle boots and with a broad, white smile, 'don't like to give the answer. But when I'm ready, I'm going. My wife and children might not. She doesn't want to think Jamaica. She feels Jamaica was against her, so she thinks England. But I'm going.'

Why should he go? 'Because back home, when you're talking to a black bank manager, he isn't going to tell you a black man can't run a business.' He has two rings and a large gold wrist-watch, a man of several parts, including real estate, 'finance' and writing for the Jamaican *Daily Gleaner*. 'I see Jamaica', he says, 'as a developing country with a lot of prospects. The only thing wrong is that they are not doing enough to encourage people to come back. I see England in decline' ('we've got to think different things apart from industry in this country'), 'with unemployment levelling out at five million.'

Would he like to see his children go back? 'Oh, Christ, yes, oh yes.' Why? 'I don't see an education system here, it's a failure. They don't get anything out of it. In Jamaica my parents sent me to school to learn. The headmaster and the teachers knew everybody, all the parents, all the children. A few who can afford it already send their kids back to the West Indies to get an education. There, they do better. There, they think more of their black kids learning. Here, the teachers do the whole Florence Nightingale thing with them: "We're here to do something for your kids, we love your kids," they say, but in themselves they think, "Oh, you're black, you can't study." It's a white system with black children.' (In addition, no less than thirty-three of Birmingham's inner city primary schools, where black children are concentrated, were built more than eighty years ago.) 'We came over in droves,' Francis continues, answering his own unspoken questions. 'One person got a house for himself, and put a family in each room. Each family has children, growing up together. They get mixed all together in the same environment, with different backgrounds. Your kids that you were trying to control just gets pulled to them others. Every day the parents have got to be telling their kids, "If you do that, I'll get the police to you." They're harder to control here, you can't control them. In

Jamaica, if a kid steal a purse, the whole village will be mourning.'

In the pool-room, lanky black youths in their woolly hats and dreadlocks are reaching over the baize as if their lives depended on it. As we pass them, Francis says under his breath that 'you won't get an education running around Handsworth. Nine out of ten, they'd be a lot better kids in Jamaica.' At midnight, out in the Soho Road, the cruising cars are bumper to bumper.

Elsa Francis came to England from Jamaica twenty-six years ago. She 'went to the factories, anywhere to get a job, to buy a few things and start myself going'. ('The Queen', she says, 'asked us to come here. She was responsible for that. We paid one-way, we were poor, we couldn't make a U-turn.') For the last fourteen years she has been working, or skivvying, in the staff cafeteria at Birmingham's All Saints' Hospital. There the other blacks say of her that 'she's had enough, she's going home'. Her husband, for seventeen years a machine operator, was made redundant (with £3,000) three years ago. Her wage is their only income, with no dole for him, since she is working. They have six children, one married, two 'living out', and three – one of whom 'got all the brain, but can't get a job' – at home in their terrace house in Hallam Street, West Bromwich.

She sits, plump and nervous, in a voluminous Saturday morning housecoat, in her front room blooming with regularly dusted plastic flowers. 'It's no good being depressed,' she says, 'you've got to make yourself happy.' She, her husband – who bolted through the back door when I arrived – and the three children still with them are returning to Jamaica early next year. She seems embarrassed, or apologetic. 'Financially we have to go,' she says, perched heavily on the sofa edge. 'My husband has went all about looking for jobs. We ain't got nothing in the bank. The house is all I have to pay my way. There's only me working, there's nothing coming from the social. What can my money do?'

The gladioli, dahlias and a potted lemon tree are all plastic.

There is a nylon-fur rug on the floral carpet, and a small white padded cocktail bar with a (disconnected) white telephone on it. 'They say because of his age,' she adds vaguely; 'we might as well go home, we'll be better off there.' How? 'We won't have to buy coats and cardigans. We won't have to pay for all this heating.' (On the front room mantelpiece stand Charles and Diana, his hand resting heavily on her royal blue shoulder, a large diamond gleaming on her finger.) She has always voted Labour. Are you tired of England? 'Not really tired,' she says wearily; 'just can't manage'.

Are you disappointed about what has happened to you? Behind her, there is a stainless-steel and glass cabinet, full of ornaments. She doesn't want to answer, eyes downcast and bosom heaving. In the cabinet are glass flying fish and a bowl of pot fruit, painted red and yellow. She fingers the crucifix at her neck, the cross she is carrying back to Jamaica. 'Because you're black,' she says, her voice muffled, as if the load on her chest was suffocating, 'you find a lot of unfairness.' How? She looks at me writing. Her husband – she told me later – had warned her 'not to get involved'. 'Where I'm working, All Saints' cafeteria,' she continues, putting the first brand to the boat she has decided to burn behind her, 'I'm the longest in the place. All the blacks are still in yellow, but it's the blacks who knows most about them jobs. Fourteen years I've been there,' she says, producing a handkerchief from her housecoat pocket and clutching it tightly, her feet in furry slippers. 'It's me who teaches them all the jobs in the cafeteria, it's me who teaches them to do the time sheets and rotas.' Feeling put upon, she is going to get it off her chest, for the record. 'For years, I was Grade nothing. I can do a bit of reading and writing, I'm handling cash and looking after the money, but they never asked me to be a supervisor – not that I wanted the job anyway,' she says proudly.

'They said, "Elsa will show you", when they were training, and when the training was done, the new ones would tell me, "Elsa, clean the floors", or "Elsa, clean out the ovens".' Why? 'Because you're black. It's a downright liberty. It's been a cruel experience.' She is making herself upset, wiping her eyes with her hankie. 'They treated me bad, that hospital. You learn them the job, and when they're finished you're still a dunce, telling you to do this and to do that, always trying to put you at the back. It's wicked. I feel very terrible about it. I look on that as colour.' If she were white, she would be flushed pink by now, with this hurt and agitation. 'And if you're daft,' she says struggling, 'you even don't know when white people is taking liberties with you. When you're black, you can be on your knees for ever.'

'I don't like to see things go down,' she says, trying to compose herself, 'I like to help out.' It has been her undoing. She says that, back in Jamaica, 'They'll be glad for me. They'll say, "Elsa and her children and her husband have come home." I think I'll be happy.' The children – though they don't, she says, see themselves as Jamaican – are 'glad to be going, God help them. If there's a job in Birmingham,' she adds, 'the whites will get it.' And if Labour were to come back to power? 'If Labour came back, the whites will still get it.' She thinks, too, that education is 'better in my country'; her 'auntie', a retired matron who stayed on in Jamaica, has two children, 'one a university lecturer, one a doctor'. Apart from her own miseries at work, she says that she 'had no troubles at all' in England. 'I don't smoke, I'm not a drinker. I don't go out much. I went to church on Sunday. I lived a quiet life, really.' As for the neighbours ('quite nice'), 'if you don't know them definitely, they don't answer. If you say hello, they don't answer.' Yet, there is 'discipline', at least, in England – 'if you're in the queue first, you know you get on first' – and 'plenty of manners'. But, she says (following her own trail from one thing to another), 'in the next ten years, there'll be more black than white round here, like Enoch Powell keeps telling. A lot of English people is emigrating, Indians taking over all the shops, taking all the business and the houses. God in heaven to tell', she exclaims, wiping her brow, 'where they getting the money.'

The years here, passing into a now familiar and resigned

retrospect, have 'just gone on and on', with 'not much to show
for them'; the situation for ever 'tight' – 'every little money I
get I spend on food' – with earnings which 'can't meet your
demands', and 'nothing coming back' from 'all the tax money
and insurance'. 'We've worked for everything,' she adds,
looking around at her cabinet, the padded cocktail bar, and the
flowers. 'We never won any money from anywhere. We was
always gambling on the pools, any tickets going we always
used to buy, but nothing ever came back all these years. I'm
just wasting my time here,' she says, eyes again tear-filled. 'I'd
have been better off if I'd never come, that's how I see it.'

'When I go around Jamaica' – she has been back recently, to
pave the way for returning – 'and see the people I left with
nothing, now they are better than we are, posh houses and
everything. And here we are, doing the work for all these
white people.' She sighs. She has lived more than half her life
in England; 'half your life is really here', is the way she puts it.
But if she had a bandanna around her head, the tone of her
tired voice could put us all in *ante-bellum* Alabama. Her
husband is a qualified baker. They will try to 'sort something
out' for themselves and set up a business in Jamaica, nearby to
Kingston. She 'will have to make friends again with people',
but it will be a 'free life', she says, compared with England;
'you can cultivate, you can get people to work for you'. Her
sister, who used to live in Luton, has gone to Canada. Her
cousin is going home too, and 'another woman in the canteen'
is also leaving. ('Many Jamaicans would return right now,' she
adds, 'if they had a roof over their heads to go to.') Then
there's the friend of her husband who 'went straight home as
soon as he was redundant'. If he hadn't, she says, cheering up
a bit, he 'would have been a patient in All Saints'. He would
have gone crackers with the conditions of life.' She says he
'slipped away from it all, from the pressures'.

'Do you think England is going down?' I ask her. She
suddenly chuckles, with her hand to her mouth like a school-
girl. 'There's no going down about it: it's gone. That's why the
Jamaicans not stopping. I'm getting out before it fall on me,

because Britain is falling down, really,' she says, at last laughing and unguarded; and, collecting herself again, 'I'm sorry for the people who I'm leaving.' When I stand up to go myself, she seems relieved. 'When you go to Jamaica,' she says, more at ease and straightening her housecoat, her eyes dark-circled, 'a freedom come over your head.' I look again at Charles's chubby pink-white hand on Di's tailored shoulder – 'young people,' Elsa says admiringly – in this black household. 'My son says, "Why do you take the money to buy that thing?" I got a telling-off when I brought it in here,' she says, laughing. 'When I leave, I might throw it in the dustbin.'

In the passage, there is a large engraving of Christ, framed in benediction – another white redeemer in a halo. 'A lot of thousands of Jamaicans are going,' Elsa tells me, coming to the door. 'Next year, it will be more. If they get help, they'll leave like bees.' Across the road is the Hallam Street Methodist church. 'Blessed Be The Lord', says the billboard, 'Who Daily Loadeth Us With Benefits.' Despite them, Elsa Francis is going.

From Uncle Sam's travel and shipping agency in Lozells, Adolph Samuda has a good view of the homeward traffic. He also has an office in Bristol, a warehouse ('We collect, or they bring to us') and 'a couple of wagons'. He is now on the road three days a week, giving estimates and collecting up household effects 'in London, Crewe, Bristol, Wales, all over'. His business is flourishing. 'We shifted six families home last week, three in Bristol, two in Birmingham, one in Manchester. We just book them and they're off, if they can afford it.' Two years ago, only 5 per cent of his custom was permanently leaving the country, for Canada or the United States, or returning to the West Indies. Since then, it has tripled; a 'dramatic increase', he calls it. 'I can see it from the turnover,' he says, sitting at his desk with phones ringing.

The market is also increasingly competitive. Ads in the *West Indian Digest* offer to 'pack containers at your door'; to ship 'trunks, barrels, cases and tea-chests, minibuses, cars, spare parts, et cetera'; to 'fly you wherever you want to go'.

There are four or five firms competing for the business in the Midlands: among them, Balu Travel, Darlington Travel – 'he do a fair bit on the Canadian side' – and Steve Aldershaw in Derby; 'I'm a step behind Aldershaw,' says Samuda. There are also 'small fry moving into the trade', and 'hustling here and there'. He quotes a figure of £2,200 for a twenty-foot container to Jamaica, and perhaps £3,600 to an island off the main route, such as St Kitts or Nevis. 'I might be able to rub it down a bit, but not much less'; though in the community you'll hear people saying that the shippers are 'making too much of a profit out of it'.

At rates like these, with fares for a family included, a returning migrant will spend all his savings and redundancy money merely getting back to where he started twenty years ago. 'A lot of people', says Samuda, 'can't make a move because they're short of money. They scrape up the fares and come in here wanting to go home' – and no wonder in this wasteland of stricken hopes, and broken or bricked-up windows – 'but they can't take their things with them, the shipping costs are so expensive. The average family wants to take the bedroom suite, the armchairs, the sofa. But they have to give their stuff away. It's heartbreaking,' he says, sitting among his invoices, the top one of which refers to the shipment of a minibus from Birmingham to Kingston.

'We don't entertain credit,' he adds. 'If they can't get the money together, they're trapped.' He used to be 'in photography', but nine years ago he began 'catching on to it. When Powell spoke, I visualized it coming. I wasn't surprised. It was facts, really.' He calls Enoch Powell, laughing uneasily, a 'prophet among his people'. Earlier, potential returnees were hesitating, 'on the bridge, deciding what to do'. Now, 'with the economic upturn in Jamaica and economic decline in Britain', they're 'getting redundancies and really taking off'. Some are 'going back for six months to see what's going on, set up somewhere and have something to hold on to'; others are leaving for good, because 'they don't think they'll ever get a fair deal in this country', and because Jamaica has 'gone back' to what he calls a 'stable form of government', after the electoral defeat of the socialist administration of Michael Manley.

Is there a mass exodus coming? He says, 'It's difficult to predict, but that's what I'm thinking. If things continue to decline here' – 'they're taking the roofs off the factories right around the city' – 'obviously you're going to have it. If things improve here, they might be tempted to stay on. But I don't believe it.' Why not? 'Because fifty per cent never intended staying.' At this point, James Hunte, the maverick – or notorious – Labour county councillor from Handsworth, unexpectedly appears in Samuda's office. He is raffish and podgy, his shirt buttons near to bursting across his belly as he wades, dishevelled, into the conversation. He thinks it a 'diabolical system' not to 'pay redundant people enough to rehabilitate themselves'; says it is a 'government responsibility' to set up 'liaison committees of community leaders, welfare officers, race relations officials, representatives of High Commissions, travel agents and shippers' to oversee ('in a co-ordinated fashion') the whole caboodle of the blacks' return from their diaspora; and thinks that 'fifty per cent of taxes' should be rebated to returnees, 'for serving Britain'.

Repatriation, Hunte says, is a 'dirty word to me'. No one has mentioned it. 'We don't understand the word in our language,' he adds belligerently, 'we want a resettlement programme.' ('When I lie in bed,' he declared later, 'I dream of Dash Valley, where I was born. I don't dream of anywhere in England.') He hectors the Lozells travel agency posters – of palm-fringed tropic beaches and dark brown naiads – with talk of money. 'Three years of social security at five thousand pounds a year, plus cost of baggage' seems to be Hunte's own rock-bottom going rate for traversing this new Middle Passage. He shouts that 'they' – the DHSS – are 'already repatriating people in a bogus system', with 'minimal' sums handed out 'on no proper basis', and 'only if you are sick, a pensioner or a pauper'. 'They are hustled off,' Samuda adds – and he should know – 'with three hundred pounds for their baggage.' Hunte accuses the Tory Party of 'only being able to think about repatriation'; but also attacks Labour, his own party ('the response we had at Transport House was like cold water') for 'standing in the way of progress', because it 'refuses to discuss with us a desperately serious problem'. In the meantime, while 'everybody is frightened of the arguments of Enoch Powell', and some West Indians are already leaving, others are 'living in hope to survive, not wanting to go back like paupers. They are here, fretting,' says Hunte. It is as good a description as any.

Yet where are the statistics to prove that this movement is occurring? A telephone spokesman at the Jamaican High Commission at first laughs warily at the word 'exodus'. 'Is that what's happening?' he asks me ironically. I tell him that it is beginning to look like it. (He hedges, asking me if I am West Indian.) When I press him again, he says that 'most people are going somewhere'; 'moving on', he calls it, to the United States, Canada and the West Indies. 'They want some sunshine,' he says, making jocular light of it. What's the scale of it? I ask him. 'They don't come to us, so how do we know?' he says, irritated. Is it large, or small, in your judgment? After a pause, 'Quite large.' Is it increasing? 'Yes.' Why? 'Because', he says testily, 'originally it was only voluntary redundancy of our people going on, now it's compulsory. The community is worried. Things are getting bad. They're seeing that people have got on better who stayed in Jamaica'; but then he doesn't want to go on talking about the subject.

'Some of the West Indians are secretive, slipping away,' says Samuda; 'they don't like trouble'. Wherever and whatever the official figures are, declares Hunte, there are so many people going that the Jamaican government has already had to impose restrictions on the import of vehicles by returnees, because of 'lack of infrastructural facilities'; a shrewd way to check the flow of people for whom a second-hand van or minibus, bought with redundancy money, would provide a means of subsistence. Certainly, about the actual scale of the exodus of blacks from Britain the Home Office and the Office of

Population Censuses and Surveys are not saying, because they don't know. This is not only because 'no information on return migration as such' is officially collected; and not only because a young black Briton is obviously not a 'return migrant'; but also because definitions of who is and who is not a British citizen – and of who is, and who is not, an immigrant or emigrant – have now become bewilderingly complex (or muddled) under the 1981 British Nationality Act.

Since 1 January 1983, the act has created new forms of nationality and statelessness, as well as dual and second-class citizenship in Britain, while intensifying all the pressures on insecure blacks to leave the country. Now, under the new rules, you can be born in the United Kingdom without being British by birth, and be a citizen of the UK without the right to a British passport. Moreover, these problems of definition are compounded by the fact that the 'new' Commonwealth countries of the Caribbean themselves devised at independence very various regulations on who were, and who were not, their citizens. But as long ago as 1975 it was being officially admitted in Whitehall that there was a 'significant amount' of 'return migration' to 'areas such as the West Indies'. Yet, today, though the scale of the movement of blacks appears to have grown very much larger (and to be increasing), there are no statistics which reveal how many people with black skins – wherever born, and of whatever citizenship – are leaving Britain.

In Hubert Tulloch's terrace barber's shop in Erdington – the Slade Salon for Ladies' and Gents' Hairdressing – it is near closing-time. His assistant is silently folding away the towels. Amid the pots of Ambi skin cream, Barnet's 'unbreakable combs', pencil sharpeners, TCB Hair-Food and Afro Folding Hair-Stylers, George Campbell, a Jamaican acquaintance of Tulloch's from up the road, is holding forth in black cap and brown anorak. Thumb-tacked to the wall above him is a *Woman's Own* souvenir supplement of the 'Christening of Prince William, Our Future King', together with the 'Bethany Christian Fellowship's' programme; and, among the magazines on a small table between us, a dog-eared copy of the *Redemption Tidings*.

'Most of my people', Campbell says, 'are country people.' When he 'set off on the boat' he was 'really young'; 'I used to say to myself, "Don't go to England." ' He arrived in October 1960 ('going on twenty-three years'), and worked as a machine operator at Hardy Spicer's – 'I was always in the union, and voting Labour' – in the Chester Road, until he was made redundant. He recalls that a 'few' of those who came over with him didn't stay long. 'As soon as they saw the factories, they paid two or three hundred pounds and went back home. Now they're settled,' he says glumly. 'But personally, for me, I didn't expect no big thing,' he adds; 'just see how things get done, get myself a little experience.' Unemployed since 1981, and 'everything against me', he has sold up, put the proceeds – including his redundancy money – into a 'little house' in Spanish Town in Jamaica, and is going back to 'do a little farming and all that'; he first, and his family later.

Do they want to go? 'They will go. All of them are ready. They might say, "This is my country." But they know they haven't got much chances.' His eldest son ('I don't know what's going to happen to him') 'don't do a thing, can't find a thing, God knows'. Yet he has his own grievances about the younger generation. 'The way I see most of these boys move,' he says, 'they didn't give themselves enough chances. A lot of this youth here, they say they hate the whites, they say the whites are prejudice, but they are lucky. The youth more and more say they're not English, because they're getting hard times here. But they're living well, compared with their parents and grandparents. Shoes, they chuck away after a day or two; food is all waste, they don't touch it. I love my eldest because he's my child, but I don't like his attitude.' Hubert listens in silence, amid the bottles of Silvikrin and styptic pencils. 'If he was ambitious, he'd jump to it. He didn't put no effort. "I won't get a job," he kept saying, "what's the point of studying at college?" ' Campbell jokingly makes as if to twist his hair into the younger generation's dreadlocks. 'To me the only reason the Rasta man do this is not to get a job. To survive as a *black* man you have to be three times better. I told my son, you have to try your best. But they don't do that, these boys give up. They could be better off, they're born in this country. But [considering it from another angle] you can't tell people to love you.'

Campbell says that 'this is a nice country; to some extent, it's not a bad country. You gain from it. You learn – perhaps some people don't – you benefit.' How? He laughs, his forehead wrinkled and anxious. 'The way to behave, the way of talking. I have a good look at the black people back home, and I say, "How am I going to live there like that?" ' What do you mean? 'They're different. I'll have to make some changes.' What changes? 'Here you go to the pub, right, and you say, "Can I have a pint of mild, please?" You wouldn't get that in Jamaica, not that way of talking and nice behaviour. You benefit in this country.' In the mirror, you can see reflected the crown of his cap and his earnest expression. 'I would love to see England come back on its feet. I don't feel angry. But there is something wrong here for an industrial country. It should be better. What you hope for just isn't here.' He is waiting only for a Jamaican permit to take his van home: 'I don't want to go back there empty-handed.'

'A lot of people going now,' he continues. 'Some people getting old, some getting browned off. You are here in this country twenty years, but you won't have money to put in the bank, as a family man. You won't have anything here in England. Everyone wants to go really, if you ask them. They expected more, somewhere down the line. I go in the pubs, in the bookies', you'll hear them. Our people are saying they are black, they are being treated unfairly.' He speaks impersonally, or politely. What about you? 'In many ways, many, many times,' he replies vaguely. 'They're dissatisfied with their treatment' – 'some of them hate the whites, especially the boys,' he added – 'the whites are getting more unfriendly. There's a lot of black people covering up. They want to say they are happy. But people is going. It's just like a sickness.

They're not really comfortable any more in this country. The racists are right,' he adds without a qualm, 'I know for a fact they're right. Two hundred and fifty thousand people will go if the government wants to give some kind of assistance. If you can't find your way out,' as he puts it, 'you should be able to go somewhere to get help. If you work in a country for twenty-five years, you should be entitled to something.' Scissors and combs are being quietly put away in a drawer.

He himself came originally for 'a quick start for five years', which turned into twenty, a mortgage and four children, debts, overtime and 'scraping'. 'You heard "London Calling" on the radio, and you thought it must be heaven. Then you got here and saw this damp, cold place with all these chimneys. Can you imagine? When I came here first,' he says, 'it was all factories, so what happened?' He leafs idly through the magazines on the table. 'Five thousand miles from home you don't know where to turn. You couldn't even raise a chicken out there, man. It's hopeless,' he says, gesturing towards Spaghetti Junction. There are not many white cocks left crowing on this dunghill, either.

'It's no good,' Campbell concludes, shaking his head. 'You want to go back, walk on the streets, happy-go-lucky. No dole, but you are free, the little things you want to do. A little land, you build a little house, one room at a time, anything you like. You pine for it.' He says he feels 'trapped', 'in a spot'. 'Home', which has made 'some rapid improvements', beckons. 'After two or three years on the social, money not easy to come by, everything begin to look different. They're saying to me, "Uncle George, come home." ' His own uncle in London, now in his seventies, says, "George, I want to go home, I want to die there." The silent assistant hangs up his white nylon overall. 'If there's a job now, I'm not taking it,' Campbell declares, yet as if still hoping against hope at this eleventh hour. 'All I want is to find myself on that plane, nothing else. I cry over it day and night that I stayed here so long.'

He suddenly seems quite ebullient, almost cheerful, pulling his cap down at the brim: 'You tell me, where is the change coming in this country, I can't positively see it.' From here, I can't either; but at least there are places left where they'll be selling pots of Brylcreem on the Day of Judgment.

When he has gone, Hubert puts up the closed sign in the window. 'As soon as I am able to,' he says gently, 'I'll be going myself. I'm upset about it, yes, but I'm encouraging people to go. Back home they can be of more value to themselves and their country. Myself, I fit in really. I've been in the Labour Party eighteen years, active in my ward, I know a lot of people, I've been a union officer, I've served on committees.' Wouldn't your going be a loss, then? He switches off the lights, and opens the door for me. 'I think it would. But life would be a lot easier, and the expense would be much less' ('when you're getting old, you need the sunshine'). 'I'd be much happier, it's a much more living community in Jamaica. It's no joke here, things are getting worse, really serious. I can't see it better. It's very hard for people, black and white, wasting away in this city.'

For the blacks, the sense of being trapped below decks as the British boat founders is growing stronger; many now crowding hopefully at the rail, and others, how many no one knows, swimming for it, back to the Caribbean.

Thoughts Among the Azaleas

June 1983

Fleet in Hampshire. It is two days after the (1983) general election. We are on the terrace of Eric Green's garden of azalea, pansy and rhododendron, deep red, pale pink, white and blue-purple. He is a marketing director, ex-Leeds University and, before that, Stretford Grammar. Flattened northern vowels are lost deep in this grove of the Home Counties. Avocado dip and bowls of peanuts stand on white wrought-iron.

Round here, in this Forest of Arden, they call their houses – with their sylvan names nailed to tree-boles – Tanglewood and Inglewood, or Woodmancote and Woodlynch; and old folks are to be found down the road in the Silver Park Lodge for Elderly Persons. The lieutenant-colonel next door voted by post from the Scillies. 'You've probably heard of Southend Refuse Services,' says Richard Barlow, in dark blue slacks, open shirt and brown slip-ons. He is framed in flowers. 'Well, that's me.' In his early forties, he comes from Chesterfield, grandson of a miner ('a fairly staunch Tory') and son of an NCB 'divisional something or other', and today making a mint out of contract cleaning. Green describes him as an 'ultra-conservative'. 'We offer a hell of a lot of commitment,' Barlow says hectically, forehead shining.

Now, in the Tory landslide – 'I'm very pleased, very' – the 'inefficient' ancillary services of the NHS beckon the privateer, nosing his way (with the help of 12·9 million voters) into the underbelly of the welfare system. Barlow's blue sweater has a small embroidered coat of arms, and the legend 'Budock Vean' on it. (Budock Vean?)

He keeps referring to Britain as 'the UK', and declares that 'we do a bloody bad job selling ourselves overseas, competing with the Japs and Germans'; says the public sector 'has had a bigger share of the national cake than it should have'; has a firm handshake, and a nicotine-stained index finger. 'I'm not saying the health service as such should be privatized,' adds Barlow, boss of Exclusive Cleaners, 'but I've a commercial axe to grind.' He says he is 'keeping more' of what he earns and is 'a damn sight better off' under the Tories. The country, he declares, has 'rejected Foot, socialism, disarmament and pulling out of Europe'.

Nevertheless, he is 'not particularly optimistic about Britain's future', or about 'reaching Utopia'. Why not? 'One,' he says on his fingers, 'because even though the Tories have been given a second chance' – 'out of apprehension about the others' – 'things have gone so far the other way in terms of discipline, the way this country's not prepared to produce what's needed, or to go out and sell in hi-tech situations, that they probably won't be able to do enough, or go far enough, to solve it.' Solve what? 'Getting our manufacturing base back,' he says quickly. 'Two, because we have too many people. And three,' fingers splayed, voice dropping, 'because you can only work within the parameters available, you can only do what is feasible, you can't turn a system on its head,' his Derbyshire accent growing stronger. His wife, Doreen (pronounced 'Dreen') is from Hull, and tells me that she works for him 'in a secretarial capacity'; 'she's my personal assistant,' says Richard, overhearing, and leaning across the glassware. Her own father – 'I come from a working-class Labour background, but both my parents have gone over' – was a foundry inspector; she has auburn hair, brown boots and a sun-tan, and is a first-time Tory voter.

'My children' – 'all my girls are Liberals, and my son is a Tory' – 'call me an arch right-wing fascist,' says Suzanne Jones, half-French and handsome, a local mixed-arable farmer's wife, laughing in a red gown, amid the crisps and olives. 'I could never be a fascist,' she exclaims in jolly fashion, 'one oligarchy and all that, it's nonsense! I'm a Conservative, I'm for freedom of choice and private enterprise. In fact, there is no commerical discipline or motivation in any government set-up. But I detest the bureaucracy which proliferates under

socialism most of all, and the frightening way everything has
been going more and more left-wing in this country.' She
means by this, 'Trotskyites and Militants getting more and
more power'. The election result, she thinks, 'offers the best
chance'. Of what? 'A reasonable opportunity for everyone.'

Of Mrs Thatcher ('I hope she's too intelligent to be
extreme, or there'd be a backlash'), she declares: 'I don't
particularly like her, and I wouldn't want to know her. But my
God you've got to admire her firmness', or what she also calls
'that shade of intransigence about her'. 'Most male criticisms'
of the prime minister she describes as 'obliquely sexist, and
that's sad. A lot of people', she adds, 'make Mrs Thatcher into
a bogeywoman. But she isn't the classic Tory woman, baying
for flogging.' Suzanne works for a local electronics firm,
'managing the office', and doesn't believe that the Tories
would 'cut the social services so deeply as to cause the poor to
suffer'. But 'if people can and are prepared to pay for anything
from schools to smoking, that's a question of freedom with
your money, of how you spend it'. She also thinks that
'western civilization is under a lot of threats', at a time when
'we need someone who knows what she is talking about, not
someone who waffles'. Under threat from what? 'The economic crisis, and over-population. We've all got these high
expectations, in world terms, which are difficult to abandon.
If we go on breeding, communism' – 'or some other appalling
totalitarian thing' – 'is inevitable. Better dead than red sounds
extreme, but the people who put it the other way round don't
know what they're saying. This is the freest country in the
world' – 'the French are more revolutionary, the British are
patient' – 'and you have to be prepared to defend what you
believe in.'

She finds the Greenham Common women 'frightening', a
'nightmare', and says that 'if they had the bomb themselves,
they'd drop it on people to convince them'. 'Glory-seekers' and
a 'laughing-stock', Doreen Barlow, chipping in, calls them.
And over the chicken in breadcrumbs and coleslaw, Farmer
Jones's wife calls equal opportunity ('a person who isn't brainy

being of equal value, and all that sort of business') a 'lovely idea', but 'it isn't human nature, it isn't realistic, is it?' In any case, she says, dark eyes flashing, her 'daily' – who has eight children and a railwayman husband – is 'red hot'. Red hot? 'She's much more right-wing than I am. She'd have all those Greenham women, never mind my opinions, rounded up by men with guns [laughing], and put in concentration camps. She thinks disarmament is crazy, and is rabid for Mrs Thatcher.'

But our host Eric Green ('I saw no future in the Labour Party') voted SDP, of which he is a founder-member. He says he is 'fairly despondent' at the election result; 'they were pulling my leg at work yesterday'. As for Labour, 'instead of being a middle party, it has this image of being dominated by left-wing revolutionaries. I don't believe it is myself, but that's how it comes across.' Do the others here today think so? 'I think they do.' Yet Tony Hancock, ex-BOAC and British Eagle, who runs an intercom business in Farnham – lives in Camberley, has his children in comprehensive schools, and knows Norman Tebbit from way back – voted Labour ('I'm immensely unusual in this setting') and thinks the election a 'total tragedy'. He comes, he says, 'from a back-to-back in Stoke-on-Trent', calls his own views 'bizarre', and 'has no contact round here with anybody who shares them'. To him, Thatcherism is simply 'small-minded': 'all about getting on and only interested in small business'. The director of a small company himself, he 'detests' it. 'I'll talk quietly,' he continues, brow furrowed, 'because there are too many Conservatives here.' The 'fundamental issue' for him is unemployment ('If she gets it down,' he says *sotto voce*, 'I'll change my colours, but she won't be able to do it'), and 'the divisions of a class-ridden society'. Drinking chilled Italian white wine in gym shoes, he says that his friends 'react badly to my opinions. No one shares them. Why I still have them I don't know myself really, but I came from a very working-class background, very. The others don't excuse me. They aren't hostile, because I'm a friendly guy, but they look on me as a

sort of curiosity, and think I should have grown out of it.'
Tebbit, whose own social provenance was a pawn-shop, is an
old buddy; Hancock describes him as 'diligent and hard-
working. He believes what he says, you can't argue against
him. He was an immensely forceful and powerful trade union
man in his Heathrow days; he did the job with professional
hostility and abrasiveness,' he adds, glass in hand and shaking
his head in puzzlement, or wonder.

Hancock's own wife, Elizabeth, ex-Birkenhead working
class, voted Tory. Out of his earshot in the buzz of animated
conversation, she says that her views are 'to the right of her
husband's. He thinks I'm a fascist,' she says wearily. 'But I'm
not pleased with the election result, not at all.' Really, why
not? 'Because it will strengthen the attitudes I dislike.' What
attitudes? 'Such as my father's,' she answers, with northern
bluntness. 'He came from a well-off Liverpool working-class
background; they kept a pub and provided me with a grammar
school education.' She describes her father's views as 'extreme, really bigoted and intolerant. As a girl I found it more
and more difficult to live with. He adopts the Victorian
values,' she continues, 'but can't understand why everybody
else doesn't. He comes from the working class, but is not
interested in people who have struggles, or who don't talk with
the right accent.' She speaks, now, with her own carefully
modulated southern exasperation; her scouse camouflaged –
or buried in confusion – in Surrey.

At the golf club, says Eric Green, taking me aside, 'the
assumption is that if you live here you couldn't have any other
thoughts than Conservatism. It manifests itself', he adds,
'when Tory canvassers come to the door. If you say something
like, "Don't count on me", just to be polite, they take a step
backward.' Most of Green's friends have 'moved to the right'.
His own wife Ann – a Lancashire lass from Old Trafford, and
deputy headmistress at a local primary school – as well as his
student son Nick ('I'm right wing'), voted Tory. 'It's the first
time', says Ann, 'that I've ever voted with conviction.'

Green himself, as I am writing in my notebook, says, 'I've

got to tell you that I admire Margaret.' Why? 'Her strength,
her will, the way she's changed her voice, the act she puts on.'
The act? 'I know it's Saatchi and Saatchi, but she's used the
facilities that are available to her to get on the right basic
wavelength.' He is himself a former BEA navigator, pensioned
off with diabetes. 'It's brilliant,' he continues, 'the way she
suggests she's thinking of the long term. People actually
believe it, they believe it in her,' he declares, fist clenched to
emphasize what he is saying. 'Another thing in her favour is
that she doesn't come from an upper-class family, but a family
of shopkeepers, drug herself up, never has a hair out of place,
and never gets flummoxed. "The girl's done well" is what
they're thinking.' This is the voice of decent (Lancashire)
aspiration, in a southern setting and a real quandary. 'Even the
bloody brigadiers and generals around here, who come from
another class' – we are only a few miles up the road from
Aldershot – 'really admire her for it.'

But when Green 'saw Foot walking' – 'waffling on, pontifi-
cating, a woolly idealist refusing to face reality, I can't think
why they chose him, it was really alarming,' says Suzanne
Jones, interrupting our tête-à-tête, crisps crunching – he says
that it gave him 'feelings of pity'. 'Poor old Michael,' he adds –
chummily calling all the politicians by their first names –
'stumbling down the steps and always having to be helped.' He
'came across as very sincere', but was, according to Green,
'basically an ill man'. Instead, 'people want strong leadership
in Britain now, a strong personality like Margaret to follow.
She's convinced people that what she said she'd do, she's
done, and they're taking the medicine. She hasn't done it, but
she's convinced them. They don't see her simply as a woman,'
he says, in blue Aertex shirt, monogrammed with his company's initials, and an expensive gold wrist-watch, 'but as
someone who'll stop the country going over the cliff, and sort
out the rotten British workman'.

His wife Ann says, 'I think we can hide behind her'; his son,
Nick, that the Labour Party should have had a 'proper PR
man', and 'got their act together. I think they'll be back, but

they need a strong leader.' 'People like to be led,' Suzanne
Jones adds with gusto, 'they want firmness of purpose.' Young
Nick is twenty-two ('I've read all the manifestos and am tired
of consensus politics'), a good golfer, and studying marketing
and economics at Strathclyde. He has a small gold crucifix
round his neck, and a very low handicap. 'The right thinks the
Labour Party has been taken over by Marxists,' he continues,
intently, 'and that the Russians are coming. I don't think it
myself, particularly, though anti-Americanism annoys me. I
went through my socialist stage for about three weeks,' he
adds, laughing. Three weeks? 'Well, perhaps about six
months, when I was having all those late-night chats at Leeds
Poly. I could understand what they were getting at all right. If
"socialism" means keeping the NHS, and looking after old
people, then I'm a socialist too. But if it means nationalizing
industry and increasing the power of trade unions, I'm flatly
against it. I wanted a Conservative victory,' he says outright.
'I was pleased that she got a landslide and a strong mandate; I
like and respect her, and I don't like Michael Foot.' ('I was
frightened of what he was going to do.') 'But I hope that she'll
be judged more strictly, now that she's got it where she wants
it. My knowledge of politics is limited, but I understand the
economics of what she is trying to do, and I don't think she's
extreme, in any way. I also believe in trade union reform,
though I don't know whether she'll be able to push it through,
that's the problem.' ('I'm starting to sound like the bloody
Tory manifesto,' he added, laughing.)

'At Strathclyde, I'm shielded from unemployment myself,'
the young man continues, 'it doesn't affect me in any way,
though I see it when I walk down the street in Glasgow. I
think "Jesus, that could be me." You must feel sorry for them,
though it's difficult for me to relate to. In any case, we're
going to have to live with it.' He calls it 'good old Milton
Friedman's "natural rate" '; and adds that 'they' – that is, the
'defeated consensus politicians' – 'keep wheeling out these
things about public works. But those sorts of jobs last five or
six years, and then you're back where you started. There just

aren't going to be enough jobs for enough people, ever.'

Richard Barlow – with his ex-working-class shoulder to the middle-class wheel of private endeavour – thinks Mrs Thatcher 'closer to my style of Toryism, from her background. I'm not one of the landed gentry, either.' (But who, or what, is Budock Vean?) She has, however, 'not been radical enough'. For his part, he would like to see social benefits cut by 50 per cent – 'it's a hard world, most people in this country don't realize it, a world of haves and have-nots. If you don't work, you starve' – cuts which would include 'unemployment pay and supplementary benefit, but not pensions', which are 'a different matter altogether'. Or, 'as quid pro quo for the benefit, these people ought to be made to avail themselves to society'.

What do you mean? 'The pendulum', he says, 'has swung too far.' He says he doesn't want to 'go back to Victorian values, the workhouse and beggars', but 'you have to have a new balance'. Such a 'new balance', however 'difficult to achieve' – because 'politicians pride themselves on their egalitarian fairness' – must involve 'a much greater willingness at the bottom end of the spectrum to do a job'. This 'balance' he also calls the 'right equilibrium', fingering his cigarette lighter, 'where the government exists for the maximum economic benefit of the maximum number of people.' There is a clatter of silver on china, and the sound of sipping. That is, for those 'genuinely incapable of existing in a competitive society, you have to have a safety net'. (The strawberries are coming.) 'But you say to the others, "Right, you'll get twenty-five pounds a week just to feed and clothe yourselves, unless you are prepared to work within the system." '

Neil Jones, Suzanne's farmer husband ('we totally disagree,' she had earlier said of him), an old Cranleighan with a second farmhouse-home in France and a degree in agriculture – his face ruddy as John Bull, and his fingers squared and heavy with his own labour – begins not to like the sound of some of this; like Eric Green, he voted SDP. 'If men's desires aren't checked,' he insists, 'it would become a very jungly world

indeed.' 'It is already,' responds Barlow, charging, 'it's a
matter of human nature.' 'It's not as jungly as it was,' says
Jones the farmer, sharply. 'Things had to be forced on to the
big bad barons. I'm in favour of free enterprise, but there have
to be restrictions.' ('But will the end result be more efficien-
cy?' interrupts Barlow. 'Yes,' answers Jones briskly.) 'The
difference between the haves and the have-nots, and the north
and south, is tragic,' Jones continues. 'It's the doctrinaire
thing I don't like. The trouble is that it's difficult to generate
passion for moderation, and for sensible solutions. But I'm fed
up with the extremes of right and left. There must be a view in
the middle.' 'Wouldn't a straightforward egalitarian politics be
more attractive?' odd-man-out Hancock ventures. 'No, no!'
they shout in chorus, laughing.

Eating with a silver spoon, while smoking, Barlow declares
that 'there's unquestionably a growing divide, but they've
asked for what they're getting'. What do you mean? 'Not more
than one million are really willing and available for work, but
don't have it. People, by way of generalization, are idle.
Two-thirds of the so-called unemployed are unemployable, or
not competitive, or drawing benefit from the state and moon-
lighting. The classic is scouse labour,' he says, deftly flicking
the ash off his trousers, 'they're virtually unmanageable. They
just don't want to work.' 'Pathetic,' comments Farmer Jones
under his breath; Barlow's manner has become more comman-
ding, and everybody listens. 'It's partly the Irish influence'; an
'attitude of mind', he calls it, 'which believes they can take on
the system and win. And you get some of the congenital
unemployed', he adds grimly, 'coming in to me for interviews
in pink hair and ear-rings.' The moment is frozen; no one at
all is smiling.

There would be no place for trade unions in his brave new
second-term Tory Britain, or 'UK', rather. 'If people want
employment from me, then as an employer I'm entitled to set
the rules and that's it. Just as I don't want somebody
representing my company – most of the CBI are a load of twits
– I don't want somebody representing my workforce either.'

He stubs out his cigarette. This must be the voice of labour, working-class vowels spreading, becoming capital; and ready now – if it can – to clean up the trade unions also.

He says, lighting up again, that the unions are a 'complete anachronism', and have 'outlived their usefulness'; 'they have no particular part to play', with their leaders 'all on their own ego-trips'. Barlow wants 'workers and management, not unions and management' brought closer together. (His wife, breaking in, calls it 'a super idea'; he says that 'labour' is 'beginning to understand it. There's a greater degree of realism coming.') Tony Hancock and Eric Green seem to have shrunk into silence. 'Everybody in our outfit has come up from the gutter anyway. If you're fair and give them a reasonable wage, they don't need a union.'

He exhales. 'But aren't you unusual?' asks Suzanne Jones across the discarded plates and the other flotsam. 'I don't think so,' he answers. 'Haven't you jibbed against the system yourself, Richard?' 'Yes, but within it,' he replies curtly. There is a silence. 'I think the union record is appalling too,' Suzanne murmurs, suddenly self-conscious. 'I don't see myself as extreme,' Barlow adds, defensive. 'It's not a dogmatic thing, "private is good and public is bad". I just believe in competition, effort and the survival of the fittest. As for comprehensive schools,' Barlow says, suddenly changing the subject, 'all that they have achieved is equality of mediocrity, not equality of opportunity.' 'Education by social counselling' is how Suzanne Jones sweepingly describes the state sector; 'if the parent abdicates the responsibility, the child should suffer for it'. 'They're a tragedy,' says her husband, Farmer Jones, sombrely; 'the worst thing that ever happened to this country,' says Barlow. His wife, Doreen, is 'vaguely guilty about private schools', but 'it wouldn't stop me sending my kids to them'. Eric Green's wife, Ann, the deputy headmistress of a state primary school, and Tony Hancock, from Farnham, keep silent.

And what about immigrant labour? ('I wouldn't call people around here racist,' Green had told me earlier. 'There might be the odd joke about it, but nothing serious. We have a Gurkha regiment up the road in Aldershot, and you see them strolling down Fleet High Street. The locals regard them as "nice little people".') 'I'm not a racist,' replies Barlow. 'I'm not particularly involved in the racial aspect of politics. I have no strong views, for example, on whether one tells the Irish to go home, and reduces the employable number of people. The black community might be their own worst enemies' – 'we've got some bloody good ones, and some awful ones' – 'but I'm not saying we should repatriate them. And I'd rather have a coloured doctor than a Sheffield layabout.' 'I agree with most of what Richard says, really,' murmurs Farmer Jones, the SDP man. 'You don't,' exclaims Suzanne Jones, incredulous, or delighted. 'I do,' says her husband; 'there's not that much difference between us'.

Richard Barlow's wife, Doreen ('I'm a bit of an ostrich'), blushes at my questions. She says that she doesn't share all her husband's views, though she voted Tory. 'A lot of our friends share them, but I have grave misgivings.' She is wearing a gold chain and bracelet. 'I'd always been a Liberal since I was eighteen. Then I met Mrs Thatcher a couple of times at Tory Party conferences, and I was so overawed,' she says timidly; 'I felt I could trust her.' 'Her complete grasp', she calls it; and tapping her pretty forehead, 'up here, all those facts and figures'. 'She's got this lovely headmistressy attitude which keeps them all in their places,' says Ann Green ('I'm tolerant on the outside, angry inside'), smilingly joining the conversation. 'Of course, she's your total fascist, she'd line them all up and bring back hanging if she could' – 'so would I,' comments Barlow, 'and we could still have a relaxed and tolerant society' – 'but she *is* so much stronger than the others.' And what would happen when the first West Indian from Brixton went to the gallows? 'To bring the riots under control,' replies Barlow swiftly, 'you'd have to use the armed forces.' 'They must abide by British rules,' says a voice, which also asks me not to identify it; 'I'd pull the lever myself on a premeditated killer. They must get topped for it.' 'But if she can't get

unemployment down,' says Doreen, becoming braver, 'she'll
be finished. I think it will go up. And with the rumblings
going on, in another five years I can begin to see the structure
of society crumbling apart. I said the other day to Richard that
it might become like a dictatorship. The way she stamped on
Pym and Prior,' she adds vaguely. 'I hope', ventures Eric
Green, 'she won't abuse her power. She might cause a lot of
trouble for herself with this "get-on-your-bike" mentality, and
crunching the unions too quickly.'

'We want a right-wing cabinet carrying out right-wing
policies,' Barlow declares, unrepentant, standing and gathering up his cigarettes and lighter. The plates are full of
picked-clean drumsticks, and olive stones. Wrought-iron
scrapes on the terrace, and Eric Green and Tony Hancock are
outnumbered.

And Budock Vean? It's the name of a classy hotel near
Falmouth, where they flog monogrammed sweaters to their
clients. 'I'm ordinary,' says Barlow, shaking hands. The
clipped lawn is bathed in sunshine. 'I don't think in terms of a
class system. I'm not working class or middle class. I'm just a
working man,' he says, in pure Derbyshire, 'a well-paid one.'
He was flying out next day to the Middle East, to help clean
up Kuwait and Saudi Arabia.

The Great Debate in Bradford

April 1984
He is a provincial middle-school headmaster, bearded and
intense, a Chekhovian figure. He is pale and grows agitated
while speaking. 'I'm a working-class intellectual. I left school
at fifteen. I'm terribly working-class. My mother had eleven
children.' Here are the aroma and sounds of school-days; bells
ringing, chalk, warmth, bodies.

'I'm angry, Mr Selbourne,' he says. He is the butt of what
he calls Bradford's 'highly tendentious race lobby'; his foes
include 'black intellectuals of aggressive disposition', who
'know little of the British traditions of understatement, civil-
ized discourse and respect for reason'. Ray Honeyford is fifty,
his beard greying, bedevilled by what he sees as the 'latter-day
McCarthyism' which pursues him; a subscriber (and contri-
butor) to the conservative *Salisbury Review*, yet who does not
consider himself to be 'particularly on the right'; brought up
as a Catholic in the Ardwick district of Manchester, and in
serious trouble.

It is a grey spring morning, in what used to be J. B.
Priestley's West Riding. There are now twenty-seven mosques
and perhaps 40,000 Moslems – out of around 60,000 Asians –
in a city, 14 per cent 'ethnic', which speaks Yorkshire,
Punjabi, Urdu, Gujarati, Gurmukhi, Bengali and Pushtu.
The multicultural air is heavy-laden with imprecations; what
is 'progress' and what 'reaction' not easy to decipher, the
dreams of some a nightmare to others. Municipal directives on
racism, culture, religion and language have divided Bradford's
teachers; with nerves strained to breaking point over disciplinary moves against them, the schools turned into battlefields. It
is the spirit of Matthew Arnold, not the *Daily Mail*, which
should be here, in these days of community turmoil.

Out in the city there are acres of abandoned Gothic mills,
doomed and derelict; 50,000 jobs have been lost in Bradford

textiles since the early 1960s. Once-great palaces of worsted
and weaving, of wealth and hard labour, they are now awaiting
demolition, or the Day of Judgment. Most are now silent
blackened ruins; with over 30,000 unemployed, 19·2 per cent
of the adult male population – and double, even triple, that
rate for Asians – and the city landscape ravaged. 'Fiercely
democratic' (and 'entirely without charm'), Priestley called
Bradford in 1933, in his *English Journey*. It was the birthplace
in 1893 of the Independent Labour Party; today, a descendant
of one of the ILP's founding members is a leading council
Tory. It was also, for Priestley, the 'true North country', 'a
tramride from the wild Pennines'; a few miles from Haworth,
Wuthering Heights and Ilkley. Today, in Bradford's Hanover
Square, the Pushtu-speaking Pathans, with their women in
full purdah, must remember their own North-West Frontier
province; birds of Empire come here to roost, or translated to
the bottom end of Manningham from the Khyber.

Recently, Imam-led Punjabis and Kashmiris – once re-
cruited *en masse* from Mirpur into Bradford textiles – marched past the Alhambra (where Irving gave his last performance) demanding halal-meat school dinners, threatened their
enemies with a rates boycott and divine retribution, and
celebrated the city council's 59:15 vote in favour of this
Moslem version of kosher with hosannas from the public
gallery to Allah; while Animal Rights campaigners – in turn
accused of being a 'bunch of racists' – marched in the opposite
direction against the Koranic prohibition upon stunning animals before slaughter. And as cuts, and more cuts, impoverish
municipal provision, the National Front runs in its own
gutters, with street-attacks and showers of school-gate leaflets
distributed by teenage skinheads, while the local political
influence of Bradford's Council for Mosques is growing. Not
to be outdone, a certain Martin MacPhee has written to the
local *Telegraph and Argus* to demand that 'caber-tossing and
the bagpipes become part of the school curriculum. I also
demand', he added, 'that haggis be served daily, pre-stunned
haggis only.'

Teachers such as Ray Honeyford at Drummond Middle are not amused. Caught up in a clash of aims, he is now stridently denounced as a 'racist' for his resistance to Bradford's education policy. ('It would be a sad day', the *Telegraph and Argus* has declared, 'if the racialist tag were sufficient to stop rational discussion.') The city fathers, with a Labour/Tory hung council and a 'high profile' policy on race relations, have seen their imperative as meeting the special cultural needs of some 20,000 'ethnic minority children' – a total which has been rising at the rate of 1,000 a year since 1977 – most of whom speak a language other than English at home, predominantly Punjabi and Urdu. In turn, the administration's critics accuse it of sacrificing a common school curriculum for all pupils to the obscurantist demands of Bradford's Moslem elders. It is a 'minefield of eggshells', as one flustered teacher put it.

Yet the city education managers, seeking to 'give parity of esteem to a resurgent Islam', will disconcertingly tell you, though not for direct attribution, that much of the conflict has been 'stage-managed' in order to 'bring the Asian community into the town hall lobbies'. It is the end result, says Mike Whittaker – the Policies Development Officer for Educational Services, and ex-Trinity College, Oxford – of what began as 'fearing a plume of smoke rising over the city'. Whittaker is described with asperity by Honeyford as 'an *éminence grise*, who has never set foot in any of my classrooms'; Whittaker describes himself as 'one of nature's Tories who votes Labour', but sounds like a white bull in an ethnic china shop.

'For twenty-five years', he says briskly, pushing the bridge of his glasses back into place with an index finger, 'the local authority could get away with letting sleeping Asians lie. Racism was a taboo subject. At the time of the 1981 riots in Toxteth, there was panic, fear and ignorance in Bradford. No one knew what was going on in the streets, no one knew who in the community to turn to. They had a ghetto-mentality; they didn't ask and we didn't give. There were no institutional bridges, no structures to negotiate with. We had to bolster up the self-respect and confidence of the community ourselves,'

he says brashly, 'and turn a few poachers into gamekeepers.'
He calls it a 'process of Asian enfranchisement', while 'making
local government goodies available to those who previously
had no share in them. Now we can cope with Moslem
demands.' You mean you've bought people off? 'Yes; and so
be it.' ('It's been remarkably cheap,' he added.)

'We have trained people to shout, provided they shout
acceptable slogans,' says Whittaker, sounding like a good
district officer in darkest India, and swishing his cane in the
manner of *The Jewel in the Crown's* Merrick. What slogans?
'Halal meat, mother-tongue teaching. The issues where we
can deliver.' And if you concede them, I ask, bowling a full
toss, it permits you to head off the agitators? 'Yes,' he says,
swiping it to the boundary, 'the alternative is separate Moslem
schools' – demanded by the Moslem Parents' Association 'in
the name of Almighty God, the Compassionate, the Merciful'
– 'and the destruction of a common education system.' That
would be what he calls the 'Catholic solution'. (Liverpool, for
example, with an old history of Orange and Green religious
rivalry, has many separate Catholic schools.) To avoid it, and
to avoid an Islamic clerisy with it, if I understand him, halal
meat has been thrown to the Moslem lions; but Honeyford's
scalp is wanted also.

Deeper into this Bradford bazaar – with its own internal
community conflicts which divide Sikhs from Moslems, Moslems from Hindus, and majority Punjabi and Urdu speakers
from the 'oppressed minority of Bradford Bengalis' – you will
find that a founder-member of the militant, but allegedly
'sexist', Asian Youth Movement, Marsha Singh, has been
given a job in the education department, advising headmasters
on how to combat racism; and that the Council for Mosques
(CFM) is doing its own British bit to keep the race relations
show on the road, as the local economy collapses. 'I've never
been bought by anyone,' says Labour councillor Mohammed
Ajeeb, who runs the CFM; 'nor is this organization a creation
of the Bradford Council'. ('Well he would say that, wouldn't
he?' Whittaker commented.) In fact, Ajeeb is one of the Asian

community's leading political brokers; declares that 'I decided the Labour Party was the party for me, my community and for Britain'; claims to 'get threats from the NF every week' and not to 'walk much in the street, even if the average British person is very liberal-minded'; and has his office wall at the CFM covered with Koranic injunctions. He represents the inner city's University Ward, where 68 per cent of the population, and 90 per cent of the children, come from the 'New Commonwealth or Pakistan'; but says that 'I don't want separatism in any form. We can't afford to live in isolation. I'm fearful of political polarization, white and black. It's not on, people can't have it even if they want it. What we want is accommodation of our cultural needs, especially in the education system.' He is speaking the same language as Whittaker, or the language Whittaker wants to hear; although with a different accent.

But it is on Ray Honeyford's head ('I began life as a Marxist, but for me Popper finished Marxism'), and on the rest of Bradford's teachers, that these political deals have been loaded. In charge of a school where 'eighty-six per cent of the children have their origins in the Indian subcontinent', Honeyford, who in his own eyes is a good man fallen among conspiring knaves and self-serving agitators, has let off steam in the *Salisbury Review*, *The Times Educational Supplement* and the local press. 'Boasting to journalists', Mohammed Ajeeb irritatedly calls it; 'crossing the Rubicon', says Whittaker, to the point where the sack beckons for Honeyford's too-public opinions. The papal bulls from Provincial House, the headquarters of the education department, and planners' edicts on equal educational opportunity, multicultural education and mother-tongue teaching, as well as in-service 'race awareness' training by what Honeyford calls 'municipal thought-police', and the monitoring and reporting of racist behaviour – racist playground jokes included – have driven him into a frenzy.

For Honeyford, it is not the job of schools to preserve and transmit 'immigrant' culture. Those who think otherwise, he argues, his forehead shining, are suffering from a 'neurotic obsession' about race relations, an obsession which is a Freudian compensation for their own racism, and is in turn producing a 'multiethnic nightmare'. It is the work of 'post-imperial liberal guilt' – 'sentimentalizing and patronizing ethnic minorities' – 'political opportunism', 'tokenism' and 'harmful colour-consciousness'; at the same time denying us the possibility of finding 'a language by means of which our own doubts, fears and aspirations can be expressed openly and honestly', as by calling a spade a spade. And without such a 'language' he claims, there is 'little hope of our coming to terms' with what he calls 'the monumental significance for our future of New Commonwealth and Pakistani immigration'.

In addition, English, he says in a Mancunian accent, is 'dying in my playground'. It is the white children in his school – now called 'indigenous' in local official parlance – who are the ethnic minority; and 'only ten per cent of the Asian children put their hands up when I ask a class how many are British'. Moreover, since the acceleration of Bradford's new multicultural initiatives in education, the standards of attainment in English seem to have fallen among Asian school-leavers, 'very few' of whom – less than 10 per cent, says City Hall – are finding jobs. According to Provincial House figures, a quarter of all children in Bradford's schools speak English only as a second language, 45 per cent left school in 1983 without any English qualification, and an alarming 30 per cent – compared with 14 per cent of 'white leavers' – left with no qualification in any subject: statistics which themselves may begin to threaten the director of education.

Off-stage, in the distance, as I talk to Honeyford at Drummond Middle, I can hear 'The Wombling Song' being sung in chorus. On his desk are education department regulations permitting an Imam to lead the Jumma school prayers on Fridays, and Moslem girls to wear 'a churidar-pyjama instead of a swimsuit in swimming lessons'. Honeyford ('I'm not a member of any party and I'm not a racist'), hounded, sees himself as a 'lone voice', 'up against an officially sanctioned and publicly funded municipal steamroller. Before that, we were an oversubscribed school, sensitive to the children's needs without being bullied into it, and getting on very nicely', in what he describes as a 'happy, friendly, multiracial atmosphere'; with a morning assembly of 'overlapping prayers' – 'I recognize all their festivals, Id and Diwali and so on' – and 'real goodwill and warmth towards every one of our pupils', until 'the authority came along with its big boots on'.

Honeyford, who has an MA in educational psychology from Lancaster, and an MEd from Manchester for work on Bernstein and the sociology of language, describes 'most educational research', Eysenck's included, as 'rubbish' – 'it doesn't stand up to the canons of scientific inquiry' – and even quotes Gramsci at me: children must acquire the capacity to 'put their baggage in order'. He means that 'the English language is the key to every child's future, Asian and non-Asian, in Britain'; to 'flourish in the culture in which the children of immigrant parents live, they must first master its language'. (In Bradford, teachers allege, a grand total of 14,500 school-going children of all ages are 'not fluent in English'. Indeed, even in its upper schools, a mere 39 per cent of 'bilingual' children are 'proficient in English'.) Thus, in what Honeyford calls 'a ruthless meritocracy', 'mastery of English' and a 'British education' are the most important means to the 'correcting of racial disadvantage'; 'little ones', he adds, referring to controversies over 'mother-tongue' teaching, 'shouldn't begin their lives in an English school by learning Urdu. Progress in England', he declares bluntly, 'is justifiably linked to linguistic competence in English.' He describes this as 'an extension of the Hoggart debate', 'but my opponents are not interested in genuine discourse'.

No, say his critics in Bradford, Asian and non-Asian, he is 'forcing Asian children to accept the majority culture'. And to do so is, variously, 'cultural chauvinism' – or, 'we know what is best for you' – 'enforced integration', and the expression of a 'superiority complex'. (The question of whether Moslem cultural loyalties will endure in Bradford whatever the council, or Honeyford, pronounces has disappeared in all the blather.) Moreover, 'we rate bilingualism highly in general,' Helen Carr, a young solicitor at the Bradford law centre, said acerbically, 'but not if the other language is Urdu.' 'Good English', they say, closing in on Honeyford, 'is a camouflage. Racism is the problem. If there's racism, it will be there, however well an Asian speaks the English language.'

Honeyford – who continually denies being a 'racist' himself – admits that 'there is a small number of racially prejudiced teachers. The vast majority are not.' 'It's in the air in many schools,' said a young woman teacher, contradicting him but anxious not to be named; 'the situation is so fraught,' she added, 'you don't want to speak about it.' Undaunted, and to make matters worse for himself, Honeyford has written in the *Salisbury Review* that 'English ambiguity and irony cannot be communicated in Urdu' – though how he knows remains a mystery – and declares, in a white heat, that 'the Asians' linguistic confusion' will ensure that they 'remain a second-rate citizenry in Britain'. ('Some day,' he adds, 'the race relations lobby will realize whose positions, theirs or mine, do more for the Asians.') And so he fervidly insists that 'the place for the preservation of a minority culture is outside the school, not in it', and, most tellingly, that 'the price to be paid for emigration to Britain is the pain of change and adaptation'. This position he describes as 'pragmatism, not prejudice', and 'based on a real concern for equality'; that is, instead of going to the mosque each evening, as many Asian pupils do, you sweat over your English spelling, and come to school next morning, preferably in uniform. Or, in Honey-speak, 'we don't want everyone looking like street-Arabs'.

To local militants, such as Riaz Shahid of the Moslem Parents' Association, this is code for 'cultural genocide': 'making children believe that their parents are old-fashioned and backward', and 'brainwashing' them into 'losing respect for their homes, their culture and their religion' – 'the identity of a person is of paramount importance. If this is lost, the person is lost.' It is the vision of a Moslem *Rake's Progress*, this, in which the victim, hopelessly ensnared, 'sinks fast into so-called Western civilization'. Instead, Shahid wants separate and single-sex schools for Asians; and, as a first step, to take over entirely and run – with Moslem headmasters – five presently Asian-dominated schools, Honeyford's among them. In these schools, 'all extra-academic activities conflicting with the tenets of Faith and forbidden in Islam' would be prohibited; Shahid's own community critics, among them wary and officially nurtured CFM Moslems, declare him to be a 'fanatic'.

But Honeyford is pallid with exasperation at such 'pressures', at the 'hysterical temperament' (an *idée fixe*) which underlies them, and at the 'dodging' of the 'real educational issues'. For him, the devout aspirations of the God-fearing count for little against the absenteeism of Asian pupils: 'comings and goings to the subcontinent', he calls it, when children are 'whisked away, sometimes for months at a time, at particularly sensitive moments in their progress'. 'Seriously interrupted schooling', he declares, 'has affected at least one-third of my pupils.' At the same time, such inconstancy 'attacks the teacher's basic source of satisfaction'. And many Moslem girls at puberty disappear from the school rolls altogether. Even Whittaker, *sotto voce* at Provincial House, described these as 'good complaints to make'; the CFM's Mohammed Ajeeb angrily dismissed them as 'wild allegations'. But the education department's own statistics reveal that there are 'fewer Asian girls than boys attending Bradford schools', and that this difference in the ratio of the sexes (about 4 per cent in the First Schools) 'becomes more emphasized as the children grow older' – reaching 15 per cent in the early teens, and in neighbouring Keighley 42 per cent at sixteen years and over, as Asian girls vanish from the education system; that they have 'gone back to Pakistan' is itself alleged by some to be a pretext for keeping them at home in Yorkshire seclusion. 'How do we in Bradford implement the principle of sexual equality,' Honeyford demands in desperation, 'when so many Asian parents don't think that education is important for their daughters?'

But why, I asked him, did you refer in the *Salisbury Review* to 'half-educated Sikhs' and 'Negroes'? (There are relatively few, perhaps 2,000, Afro-Caribbeans in Bradford.) Why use such language? 'Why not? I have anger in me,' he answered. 'Disgraceful,' said Phil Beeley, the Labour leader of the city council. 'Distasteful,' said Peter Gilmour, the 'left' Tory chairman of the Bradford education committee – himself abused by the outside-right, and under a cloud as bipartisanism staggers. 'Unleashing the genie of racism and hatred, inciting white people and undermining the culture of our children,' said Councillor Ajeeb. (And, added Ajeeb, for good measure, Honeyford is 'trying to represent the lower working class, the white proletariat'.) 'Anti-black' and 'flouting the policy of the council', said Whittaker and Marsha Singh in chorus. 'Making ethnic minority children the scapegoats for all that he knows is wrong with inner city education,' said Alex Fellows, who teaches at one of the specially provided language centres which give 'extra help in English', mainly to Asian children. Even the National Union of Teachers has called for Honeyford's resignation. 'He is a hard-line racist and very clever right-winger,' says Barry Thorne ('I'm actually a Christian'), a British Telecom engineer from Keighley. Chief whip on the council, and one of Labour's main spokesmen on race in Bradford, Thorne bravely admits that 'racism is more predominant in the working class than the other classes'. But 'if I want to wear a turban', he continues, summing up his own position on race relations, 'why should there be a hassle? I can't get worked up about halal meat, or Moslem burials either.' As for Honeyford, 'anybody who can write for *Salisbury Review* is either bloody thick, or knows what he is doing. And Honeyford's not stupid.' ('The trouble is,' I was told at the education department, though not for attribution, 'he's much more intelligent than his critics.')

'It upsets me terribly,' answers Honeyford, perspiring, 'for people to allege that I'm a racist.' He calls it 'plain silly', and the 'language of totalitarian thinking'; lamenting, the while, the problems of 'living in a city which cannot tolerate dissent', his own dissent mainly. 'In fact,' he continues, 'I don't fit neatly into any of the categories they throw at me. I agree, for instance, with what Tony Benn says about the manipulation and inadequacy of the media. By abusing and hounding me, people think they're grasping the bull by the horns, but the real problems of education in Bradford have nothing whatever to do with racism. The trouble is that they know their arguments are unsound,' Honeyford (with sweet reason) argues, cornered – 'pressure will mount on him,' say his foes, with unconcealed relish – 'but they can't bear to be told it. If you don't accept their race-speak, you're the enemy, or a racist.' 'Attacking the cant' is what he calls his own belligerent declarations; and adds that one of his school governors, an Asian ('who speaks very little English, and can't read it'), 'came in yesterday and said to me; "Can't you say you're sorry?" I told him "I'm not sorry." ' 'Then if he has the right to say what he is saying,' replies Ajeeb, 'I have the right to say he is a racist.' Oh, come back Arnold, come back Ruskin – even Hoggart – and give your own verdicts on Bradford's bitter dissensions.

'We're overriding teachers' objections,' Mike Whittaker told me in a pub around the corner from Provincial House. 'Moslem demands are just, and I'm a municipal hatchet-man, not part of the race relations industry. We're simply not allowing teachers to run their schools as they see fit. The smack of firm government', he says, laughing – a true *pukka sahib* – 'has ruffled their feathers.' Honeyford, white about the gills, in his turn seizes hold of the work of the educationist Maureen Stone with the enthusiasm of a man drowning. 'The school system', he says, quoting her, eye glinting, 'has never "reflected the culture" of the majority of children in this country who are working class. Why then this concern to "reflect the culture" of small sections of that class?' Now, there's a question for you; and, sighing, Honeyford adds that 'life is full of ambiguities and complexities. But to them there's no position between being a member of the National Front, and being fully committed to their ideas of multicultural education.'

'Most of the teachers are with Honeyford,' announces Shirley Woodman – 'totally disillusioned' with a 'sick authority' – at Netherlands Avenue Special School in Wibsey. Another assailed Bradford head, she is secretary of the local branch of the National Association of Head Teachers, which, she declares proudly, is helping to lead the 'professional backlash' against administrators who are 'compromising teachers' independence'. 'I'm Leeds Jewish,' she says, bristling and lithe in a dark grey suit, white blouse with black buttons, sling-back shoes and black stockings; 'they can't talk to me about racism, I grew up with it'. ('They' can, and they do.) Supported discreetly by the right-wing Labour Lord Mayor, Norman Free, as the multiracial stew thickens, she has St George and the Dragon, and the Union Jack, on *her* school walls; and the children, black, white, brown and sky-blue pink – 'one big happy family' – dressed up as Puritans in a school-play which has become a veritable Passion. Fond of walking the dales with the West Riding Ramblers' Association, and a member of the Leeds Thespians, 'Do you think, be honest,' she asked, 'that we're being unreasonable, as teachers? I'm not going to be a little mouse, my personality has to come out when I protect myself,' she added, her eyes heavy with eye-shadow and her dark hair cascading. After a *Daily Mail* article quoting her own opposition to 'race awareness' courses for teachers – 'sniping in the press', Whittaker called her comments – she has received a *'Verdampte Jude, Sieg Heil, Adolf Hitler'* postcard scrawled to her from Nottingham, on the one hand, and a compensatory invitation to join the New Britain Party, on the other. 'We were an ethnic minority too, but the education system didn't undermine my culture,' she says, trying to put the lid on as the steam-pressure rises.

No matter; on Moslem parental rights, on Moslem sensibilities, on racialist behaviour, Whittaker says, 'We told the

teachers, "You will, you must, you have to, or face disciplinary proceedings, like any other council employee or servant."
At the end of the day, teachers are our line-managers. Their
job is to see that what we want is done. They may not be used
to being talked to in this way, but we're not just paying their
salaries and ferrying exercise books and chalk around the city.'
He describes Bradford's race relations policies as 'imposed
from the top, bipartisan, consumer-led and open-ended'; and
a 'justification for local government' into the bargain. 'There'll
be no retreat,' he proclaims, as the tempo quickens. 'The
region of stone walls,' Priestley called the old West Riding;
'when I see them, I know that I am home again,' he said
finely. But whether he would have recognized the ones which
now run through the centre of Bradford is another question.

In Durham Road, white working-class mothers gather in
their houses to give battle in defence of Honeyford and the
outrages he has committed against municipal Islam – a mutant
form of the municipal socialism of the old days. Pauline
Sawyer ('they get grants for everything, them Asians, Labour
supports them'), a non-teaching assistant at the Lilycroft First
School, is in her parlour clutching yet another draft letter to
the Bradford *Telegraph and Argus*. She says she was 'booed
out of the Drummond school hall' – 'they were all talking
Asian, really aerated' – at a recent meeting to discuss the
current shemozzles. Liz Green, a dinner lady in blue eye-
make-up and a last-time Tory voter ('but the Tories are no
better than Labour with all these Asian voters'), calls it a
'disgusting situation'.

'We've needed someone to speak for us for a long time,' Liz
Green says. 'Now Mr Honeyford's done it. If they really sack
him, there'll be uproar. Can we take *them* to the race relations,
that's the question?' What exactly is disgusting, I ask her?
'They daren't speak out, everything is racial, and booking
them for it.' What do you mean? 'The Asian girls and boys,
with all this reporting, say to the whites, "I'll have you for
racial", and now they can't answer.' The decent terrace house
swells with indignation. 'We're not racialists,' say the voices in

chorus, necks flushing, 'in no way, our friends are married to them,' they shout, laughing. 'It's inciting us to be racial, really getting people going. We all want to get on and live together. Colour doesn't come into it. It's the balance. It shouldn't have gone over 50:50. It's ninety per cent at Drummond.' Nineteen schools in the city of Bradford have more than 70 per cent of 'bilingual' children, where the 'white ethnic minority', as Honeyford slyly describes it, is 'overshadowed'. Indeed, two schools in Bradford have 100 per cent 'bilingual' children; another four, 90 per cent or over. 'I've had two girls under Mr Honeyford,' says Liz Green, 'and you just get so boiled up about it.' ('It's real, the problem,' even Helen Carr at the Law Centre conceded: 'you'll hardly see a single white kid going into some of the First Schools. Who are we to judge the white parents?')

You can hear the tide of Islam crashing down here, and flowing through the terrace houses. 'They should give them the food they want, but it's one demand after another,' says Pauline Sawyer. 'They go to the mosque in the evening, and that should be enough for them. They should leave it out of the schools, that's what we're saying.' In the hearth is a miner's lamp for ornament, and a bowl of yellow roses, in plastic.

'They don't even want halal,' says Liz Green, who, as a dinner lady, is in the front line of it. 'They love fish fingers, chips and peas, you see them looking at it. They want to eat our food, so why shouldn't they, if they want to?'; while the taboo on touching pig-meat, and the refusal of the local trade unions to permit special conditions of service, chokes off Moslem recruits who could otherwise help dish out the various hot dinners. 'It's the old men from the mosque, telling everybody how to vote, telling the women to stop at home, interfering in everything. They say we have no morals in England, it's insulting, won't let the youngsters mix or go dancing, and them with more than one wife, marrying their cousins, all that interbreeding. I think it's disgusting, I do, disgusting.'

'There's been no bombs dropped as yet, but we'll just be like Northern Ireland in the end, it's all religion,' chips in Mrs Billadeau. She is a home-help, but has no Asian customers; 'they look after their own,' she says, 'they're better than what we are, they cling to one another. Our Scott', she goes on somewhat louder, 'hasn't got a clue. He's eight. He's at Whetley Lane, flooded with Asians, all speaking Paki, and he came home the other day, and asks me, "Who were Mary and Jesus?" I don't go to church, but I'm having to learn him myself,' she says in the mother-tongue, 'it's shocking. They know all about Diwali, but what do they know about Christmas, that's what I'm saying.' 'They'll have to learn English and English ways,' say the female voices in a blur of simultaneous indignation. 'When I'm trying to learn them something and that child speaks Urdu,' Pauline says, even louder – shouting down Mrs Billadeau's 'Don't get me wrong, I like to learn about other religions' – 'I can't understand it. If I say, "Don't speak Urdu", I get told off for it.' 'And more so because we're women,' says Liz in the clamour. 'They won't listen to women'; 'you get that from children this high'; 'when they've been back to Pakistan, they're like animals, they're atrocious'; 'if you ask a child what they said, you get a three-way conversation going, you can't get any sense out of them,' declares the Babel. 'In the finish, they swear at you in Urdu,' they say all together. 'They're not chastised, the boys aren't,' says Liz, 'they've got no behaviour patterns. The boot's on the other foot.' What boot? 'They're more racist [ah!] than we are.' This is more than ruffled feathers; even the flying geese on the front-room wall seem to be honking. And to cap it all, they are in favour of school uniform: 'it stops all this competition', 'it makes all people equal'.

Up the Great Horton Road, you pass in succession the Shimla Sweet House and Take-Away, the Bank of Baroda and the Shearbridge, a Tetley boozer with its sign a florid drinker, quaffing his Anglo-Saxon ale in riding pink and monocle. The passers-by in the cold, blustery rain are mostly Asian. A few yards up, at the junction with Back Laisteridge Lane, 'ACID IS

SUPER' is spray-painted on a salami manufacturers' street-corner wall; chocolate Easter chicks, tinsel-wrapped in a gloomy shop-window, are ranged – at £2.79, £1.49, and fifty pence – in their own pecking-order. Here, the skyline is of the derelict, silent mills; and around you are the dour ruined terraces, stuck with Urdu bills and posters ('Afia Begum Will Stay!'; 'No More Deportations!'; 'Smash Racism!'). 'All corners', was how Priestley described Edwardian Bradford, 'hard, provincial corners'; but harder now than ever. In a nearby cobbled ginnel, which leads only to a waste of dereliction, of dumped mattresses and rusting iron, uncollected black plastic bags spill out their rubbish in a trodden mulch of oozing cardboard and chucked-out carpets.

In 1933, Priestley, looking back to 1914, himself lamented how 'miles of semi-detached villas had been built where once I rolled among the gigantic buttercups and daisies'. Today, many of these villas are themselves condemned housing; and fifty years on from his journey, the flora and fauna of the run-down streets are Asian. The buttercups have become kebabs and the daisies chapatis, in an urban wilderness as bleak as anything in Britain. The housing stock in these slums is justly described by local community and social workers as a 'total disaster', with conditions ('thirty Asians sitting around a gas-fire sharing a cigarette') 'desperate': a world of halted improvement grants, and of no new council building; of Asians not wanting to live on 'white' council estates, and of housing associations 'not interested in Asians'; of multi-occupation – 60 per cent of all Asian households, and 10,000 households in total, are officially 'overcrowded' – and grey swathes of demolition.

So, too, as the local economy goes under, the welfare network of public and voluntary provision, overlapping with and woven into the education sector, spreads across the city to replace the old world of production. It is a labyrinth of casework agencies, family service units, and neighbourhood advice centres; a jungle of mutual dependencies between the providers and their clients, known as the welfare system. And that in a local textile-formed culture, proud – a women's pride most often – of its working-class traditions of self-reliance. The Bradford law centre works for Asian tenants and against rack-renting Asian landlords; the most conscientious of Bradford's servants – teachers, social workers and health visitors among them – now learn Urdu; forty-four Council for Mosques' 'advice workers', funded by the Manpower Services Commission, are available at local mosques to give advice on 'where to go for welfare benefits, housing, education, social services, nationality and immigration, etcetera'. ('Fifty to sixty per cent of Asians are unemployed,' Mohammed Ajeeb estimated; 'at the least, not less than half, one way or the other.') The social services department, the Community Relations Council, the Council for Voluntary Service, the Citizens' Advice Bureau, the Child Poverty Action Group, the Asian Woman's Centre, Gingerbread, and a dozen other agencies toil in the same thankless vineyard: of urban decay, tangled welfare regulation, jesuitical immigration rules, fuel debts, marital problems, wishful thinking, and slowly rising unemployment; while in the inner-city warrens run Asian hustlers, penmen and barrack-room lawyers, charging their own community members for services obtainable free from this or that welfare office.

Yasmin Rifat, the young Pakistani 'advice worker' at the Citizens' Advice Bureau, a former nurse, speaks English with a broad Yorkshire accent. 'My grandad is buried in Newcastle,' she says; 'my dad is a textile worker in Huddersfield, and my mother was thirteen when she married.' ('I'm quite westernized,' she adds casually, 'but part of me, the part I'll keep, is Asian.') Her beat is 'housing benefits, immigration, consumer problems, unfair dismissals, and matrimonial'. Multicultural welfarism, in this Pennine Punjab, is a coloured (but fading) rainbow of provision: this morning's clients have included an Asian girl resisting an arranged marrige to a Bradford Pakistani widower with complex child-care problems; a wife-beating Pakistani husband from Little Horton who has left his family without financial support to 'set up with a white woman'; and 'a white woman married to an unemployed Asian who has disappeared to Karachi with their children'.

Yasmin's friend, Anne Perkins, a social worker, speaks a modest Urdu herself and is today vicariously hot under the collar about the fostering of two Asians in a 'white home', because 'they will lose their culture'. She claims to be 'teaching them the language they have lost'. It seems a veritable transmigration of souls. 'Some of the younger Asians,' she says with scorn – over her curry in the Lumb Lane Sweet House – 'want to be more English than the English.' Meanwhile, across the city, Ray Honeyford, chased by what he calls 'diktats', writes to *The Times Educational Supplement* denouncing as the 'worst kind of patronizing tokenism' attempts to 'teach an immigrant culture by those' – like Anne Perkins – 'manifestly not part of that culture'. And at the heart of this tangled web of social action are the same old raucous accusations of everybody else's racism; of Asians and whites alike fiddling the system; as well as the dependants' jargon of 'sup.-ben.', 'case-loads', social security guidelines, appeal tribunals and overdue, or underpaid, 'giros'. But it is all a propping up, and patching up, and covering over of the true lineaments of things, and the direction events are taking; less a welfare state than a welfare civil society, in which the multiracial 'struggles' of the clients of the state and their 'expert' advisers – struggles for everything from an Asian Women's Hostel to (mosque-demanded) 'naked flame' gas cookers, and against everything from electricity disconnections to deportation – have become a parody of productive effort; a maze, in which 'enterprise' searches the small print of DHSS leaflets, and 'hard work' secures a disputed hand-out. Indeed, in places like these, where the old social order is dissolving in squalor, dependency and unemployment, the battle for 'benefits' has itself become a (mutant) form of class conflict.

In the decline of the inner city, a gibe is made or a job is lost, and the act is monitored and the statistic collected. The fine art of 'ethnic head-counting', authorized by Bradford's post-Raj planners, can even tell you the proportion of bacon-eating Hindu children (67·6 per cent), and how many young Sikhs – for whom halal is itself forbidden – eat chicken (92·6 per cent). This is 'mandatory' toleration and 'parity of esteem', expressed in mathematics; or the algebra, and abracadabra, of equity and 'balance'. And in City Hall – partly closed because of extensive dry rot in its timbers – the local politicians on the high-wire uphold the principles of the 1944 Education Act on the one hand, and the Slaughterhouse Act of 1974 on the other; while seeking to avoid the communal booby-traps that race sets for the wary and unwary alike. In the vote on halal, thirteen of the fifty-nine in support of it were Tory; but even Whittaker conceded that 'council policy rests on shaky foundations'.

For there is as much conflict deep within the parties as between them. Thus, the 'need to reflect the anxieties of the indigenous [sc. white] population', the growing political clout, in many wards, of the Asian voter (for whom, it is said, 'owner-occupation is next to religion'), the fear of a working- and lower middle-class Tory backlash against the 'wetter' representatives on the council, and the Friedmanite issue of the 'rights of Moslem parents' under the Education Act, have between them let loose several multicoloured cats among the Conservative pigeons. And behind the sterile Labour scenes, the ranks of councillors, some much less 'progressive' than their Tory opposite numbers, have their own domestic problems; the Labour-voting 'anti-immigrant' constituency on the council estates not the least of them. 'When in Rome,' the Labour Mayor, Norman Free, told the Moslems in the great debate on halal, 'do as the Romans, or pay the difference'; portly in his chain of office, he was whisperingly described to me by some of his left-wing colleagues as a 'nutter'.

But in public at least, and in the panelled council chamber, most Labour councillors seem firmly in favour of Honeyford's removal. 'Socialists', says the Labour leader Phil Beeley – who also speaks bitterly of the 'dismal wreckage of people on the dole in this area' – 'must make sure that the cultures and

religions of the various communities are respected.' Yet, in
private and unbuttoned, it becomes much more convoluted.
'Honeyford shouldn't be treated as a racist,' says Councillor
Derek Smith, a former Labour leader and now secretary of the
Bradford Trades Council. 'It surprises me that his sacking has
been called for. If he's made points,' as he puts it, stolid and
quiet, 'they should be investigated. In Bradford,' he continues, seeming to savour the word's hardness, 'you've got to
take people with you. There's far too much concentration on
race issues.' (Even Beeley complained, behind his hand, that
the 'local authority can't go round interpreting the Koran'.) 'A
lot', Smith declares simply, 'think white working-class interests are being neglected. I hear it all the time,' he added, 'on
the buses.' 'The kind of thing racist whites say,' according to
Maggie Pearson, a voluntary worker with Gingerbread, 'is
"social security treated me like muck. If I'd been a Paki, they'd
have treated me like the bloody Queen Mother." ' 'You can't
eradicate the prejudices and instincts of Bradford folk,' Smith
says flatly, as if that were – and perhaps it is – the end of the
matter.

And John Senior, another former Labour council leader,
ex-Lord Mayor, and an 'energy salesman' with the local
electricity board, is in favour of halal meat, yet refers with
distaste to the 'long pantaloons' of the Pakistani. 'Two children of different races', he says, 'should be allowed to eat what
they want at a school dinner-table'. But through the side of his
mouth he talks about the need to 'keep a tight hold on things in
an interim race situation', instead of 'fiddling money away on
community work. One thing you don't bloody want to do,' he
continues, 'when the racialists are crawling out of the woodwork, is to pretend you're more bloody Pakistani than the
Pakistanis. Even if you do, they don't respect you.' As for
Honeyford, 'If I was a headmaster, and I'd got some of those
bloody orders he's got, I'd have shoved 'em . . . [laughing]
. . . in the eye of the bloody director of education.'

Supping his ale from a silver tankard at the East Bierley
Cricket Club – with not an Asian in sight, and the 10 p.m.

darts flying behind him – he calls himself an 'old-fashioned socialist'; 'I wanted to change the fucking world overnight myself,' he says, wiping his mouth with the back of his hand, 'once upon a time.' (Local Labour's young turks, in a bitterly divided party, call him 'a piss artist'.) He claims that 'each mosque in Bradford has its own bloody leader, like the Catholic priests, to make sure the bloody Koran is stuck to. The youngsters are beginning to rebel, but it'll take a bloody generation before there's enlightenment among the Asians,' he says confidentially; 'and I'm not talking bloody book-rubbish, neither,' he added.

Meanwhile, the race-planners, much of their authority resting upon the fact of an evenly divided council – which necessarily devolves power to officials – continue to lean over backwards on 'ethnic' issues, only to get further up people's noses. It is a manoeuvre worthy of Tantric yoga. In pursuit of what they think is enlightened self-interest, they are in fact getting tough with the (white) natives, while endorsing the Asian community's control over its own younger, 'westernizing' generation. Dafter still, they are accommodating Islamic reaction – hostile to coeducation, sex education, health education, women's emancipation, 'Christianization', mixed drama, mixed gymnastics, mixed swimming and mixed dancing – in the name of 'good race relations'; and even, some of them, in the name of 'socialist' progress.

But this is not the politics of the nineteenth-century Bradford Nonconformist, or of the Victorian liberal merchant; nor the politics, either, of that 'curious leaven of intelligent aliens', as Priestley called the German and German-Jewish settlers of an earlier textile immigration. It is the mullahs' Islam of north Pakistani villages which has come to Bradford, a provincial Yorkshire city, in its darkest hours of economic failure. Indeed, it is the village Islam of a quarter of a century ago which Bradford's Imams are trying to hang on to, an Islam remembered from the days of the exodus to the West Riding. It is backward even in the Indian subcontinent's own terms, with its moral preferences for conscious cattle and uncon-

scious women; but if, in the Bradford Asian community, there
are many who know this, there are few, or none, who will
admit it.

And so the planners plough on, duped by the kerfuffle,
though increasingly uneasy. 'Education in Bradford', say the
city's administrators, 'is working at the frontiers of experience
and knowledge.' It looks as if the demand for Moslem girls to
keep their clothes on in the showers has got them really
flummoxed.

In the Trenches of South Yorkshire

January 1985
'If I saw Arthur Scargill,' says the Welsh woman, singsong, 'I would, I'd throw this at him.' 'This' is her BR tea, steaming in its plastic-lidded Maxpax. She cackles good-humouredly, white-haired and hard of hearing, amid the Cadbury's Roses, light snoring and McEwan's lagers, as the train pulls out of Derby. 'My father was a Welsh miner, died of pneumoconiosis, and my brother, but they never done like he's doing.' No one demurs – the class struggle being at a low ebb in a fug like this – knitting-needles clicking over the Twix bars and dog-eared *Mirror* sports pages; other heads wired-up to personal stereos, eyes glued to the 'teen magazine' *Smash Hits*, and fingers in the Golden Wonder, Ready Salted.

But then, in the First English Civil War (if the coal strike is a familiar token of the Second), the Derbyshire miners themselves were mostly for the Cavaliers, not the Roundheads, with 'not a dozen Levellers among them'. It was the mine-owners and local gentry in these parts who were parliamentarians. And stuff today's talk of 'martial law' in the coalfields and 'siege policing' (*Socialist Worker*); consider instead that a poll for 'the most important event of 1984' in *Smash Hits* – lent to me as we pass Sheffield's rusting and dismantled steel mills, where the bulldozers are sweeping clean, for acres – has voted Duran Duran drummer Roger Taylor's wedding (top) and Wham! guitarist Andrew Ridgeley's nose-job (third), way ahead of the miners' strike (eleventh). Twelfth by a short head – and a lower forehead – was Boy George's new hair-colour.

Thirteen years ago, in an earlier and more benign phase of this pit, or trench, warfare, the generals were the TUC's homely Vic Feather, that nice Derek Ezra at the Coal Board, the wettest of wet Tories at the Department of Employment, Robert Carr, and Uncle Joe Gormley at the NUM. Wilson –

like Kinnock – put his head under the winter blankets, the 'intransigent' Heath 'sweated it out' in the press headlines, the Stock Exchange cheered as the FT index crossed 500, and the jobless figures 'soared' to one million. But in those days the army of miners was more or less united, the press more or less sympathetic, the siege and fall of Saltley Gate in 1972 – with young Arthur Scargill in the thick of the action – a trade union Bastille Day; and Mrs Thatcher was Minister of Education. Today, foes are dug in deeper, the miners (and police) divided among themselves, the social prospects darker, the honours more than ever pyrrhic. Today, too, in conditions of deepening economic decline, issues of the right to work, in all its meanings, public order and trade union freedoms, police powers and community well-being – as well as the question, what is reactionary and what progressive? – fall as shadows across the whole political spectrum.

At Doncaster, with its strike-hit town traders, its eleven pits and 18·5 per cent unemployment, the local *Star* ('Beautiful Sight As Pit-Face Starts Up'; 'Miner Dies Delivering Gifts of Coal') is itself schizoid. But then Scargill's slow-motion kamikaze act has been a complicated as well as a costly process. On one page, it's '£1 million a week to police the pit dispute in S. Yorkshire', according to George Moores, the county council police committee chairman, for a grand total so far, in South Yorkshire alone, of £36,838,750. On another page ('Help Out For Pit Punch-Up'), *working* miners at the Yorkshire pit of Shireoaks 'are using their pay packets to bale out a colleague convicted of hitting a striker'. On a third page, there's the 'Optimism of Life on the Picket' at Brodsworth. But among the letters, Sheila Staniland from Oughtibridge – whose own husband has been 'out of work for four years' – complains bitterly ('I can't keep my feelings to myself') about the '£30 Christmas hamper' local striking miners are said to be receiving from their support-funds. 'I can't see', she writes, 'why they can get it, when we don't get a thing at Christmas.' And if you can't face any of it, cuddly Russell Grant – bottom of page two – offers to Doncaster Taurus readers 'money bonuses, with a loved one handing you a fiver or two'; to Cancers, 'festive froth and fun all round'; and to Capricorns, 'a brand-new direction'.

But up the High Street and into the Ho-Ho Chinese restaurant, near-empty, with its wave-like ruched curtains and orange goldfish mouthing in the bubbling fish-tank, watery-eyed Eddie from Armthorpe and little Eric from Cantley are up to their own Yuletide gills in boozed-up anti-strike and anti-police banter. They are both NUR men ('the strike's crippling t' bloody railways'), both twenty-seven, Eddie with a wife and two children. 'The Met police,' says Eric, tongue thickened, 'if you sneeze, they'll fucking frisk you.' On average, each day, there are around 2,000 outside or 'foreign' police in the county, the hated Met among them; accused locally not only of violence ('handing out a spot of fist', 'truncheoning', 'spitting', 'kicking'), but also of 'goading and taunting' the strikers – 'throwing coins' and 'waving pay packets' at them – and 'cheering the injured'. 'Send 'em back,' says Eddie, into his tipple. 'And I', he says, suddenly stabbing his own chest, jacket off, with his fingers, 'call 'em fucking pigs, and my own brother's a policeman.' The Ho-Ho staff, assailed by the effing and blinding, stand unblinking beside their bottles of soya. 'We had a copper in Armthorpe,' says Eddie – 'Eddie's getting back to his childhood days now,' says Eric – 'he knew everybody in the village. He'd either tell your dad, or give you a belt round the ear-hole. I respected him, I'll tell you. But if I saw a copper on the floor now,' says Eddie, white-faced with drink, 'getting the shit kicked out of him, I'd walk away and say, "Oh, fuck him." Or I'd stick the boot in meself,' he says laughing.

'Aye, but away from t' mining villages, Eddie, they say they're doing a job, that's what they're saying,' says Eric. 'If they sat on crimes as hard as they've sat on fucking miners, they might get summat sorted out,' says Eddie. 'There's a fantastic feeling in the soup kitchens,' John Healy, an NUM electrician from Balby, and a Labour county councillor, told me later. But here in 'Donny', among the South Yorkshire

chow meins and prawn chop sueys, it's not so much pints of
bitter as gall and wormwood.

For Eric and Eddie, Scargill is also a target of venom –
'don't get me wrong,' says Eric, 'I'm an ordinary working man.
I support the miners' – with his 'chauffeur driven Rover'; and
'another fucking Rover of his own [with a fierce two-fingered
'up yours' gesture] that he doesn't bring out of his garage'.
'There's miners who haven't got a fucking tin of beans out of
this strike, but the top nobs are not going short, none of 'em,'
says Eddie, head bobbing. As for the 'miners on the gate'
outside the British Rail engineering works in Doncaster,
'rattling their tins at us, and saying, "Come on, lads!", how do
we know if they're miners?'

There is a plague in the Ho-Ho on everybody's houses; 'and
the rest of 'em, pestering us with Marxist papers'. 'I've not
donated nothing to the miners,' says Eric, screwing up his
eyes, the booze now making him meaner. 'When you put your
money in them buckets, you don't know if it's going to the
families' – 'if it was going straight to 'em, I'd give 'em all my
wages' – 'or [with an unsteady sweep of the arm] that bloody
Militant Tendency, or to run coaches to the picket lines.'
'Anyroad, it's all Scargill versus Thatcher,' say Eric and
Eddie between them, talking each other down, 'the miners
are just pawns, nine out of ten of 'em 'd say the same if
they were truthful, they've nowt to do wi' it.' Subsiding, they
shake their heads over their glasses ('there's a lot of unease,
isn't there, Eddie?' says Eric), bravado undermined, and
ebbing.

'We'll always make good of a bad day,' says Eric, maudlin,
'but the friction over the miners is something terrible at our
place' – British Rail Engineering – where for four recent job
vacancies there were 'five hundred fucking applications'. 'But
they're fighting a lost cause, they've lost it, and that's it,
Eddie. They lost it from that second week, when they should
have had a ballot.' 'They've lost it and they don't want to
admit it,' says Eddie. 'They can't win,' says Eric. 'They won't
win,' says Eddie. 'I hope they do win,' says Eric. 'They can't,'

says Eddie, flatly. *Smash Hits* placed King Arthur sixth in its 'Prat of the Year' contest.

On the road to Barnsley with County Councillor John Healy – fifteen pence for a forty minutes' subsidized bus ride in the 'socialist republic' – we pass through Grimethorpe, busy with its shopping. Together with the previous year's 'cavalry charges' at Orgreave and the battlefields of Kiveton and Armthorpe, Grimethorpe will always be remembered, says Healy, for what he calls its 'horrendous clashes', riot gear and police beatings, as the First Civil War's Marston Moor and Edgehill are remembered, or forgotten. 'This is where the police came down,' he says, pointing out of the steamed-up window. 'Once the two pits here go, the community goes down with them.' Highgate pit's winding gear may still be unmoving as we pass, but there are wheels turning within wheels for all that. On the one hand, Healy says, a local Tory magistrate, a Mrs Cuttriss, has agreed with him in public that 'the long-term prospects for local policing' are 'disastrous'. ('It floored me that did,' says Healy.) On the other, 'we, the NUM, have blasted local labour movement JPs for being so severe with bail conditions for arrested miners. They uphold the rules, exactly the same as the Tories.'

Two miles past Grimethorpe, Healy alleges that the police have not only been fattened up with overtime – 'like Christmas turkeys', as a striking miner described it that evening at the Askern Miners' Welfare – but, 'they're going into the picket lines to get themselves hurt, they're getting that much compensation.' So far, 1,200 police have been injured in the strike, at an estimated likely cost of £1·5 million. 'Shooting themselves in the foot,' Healy calls it. Together with Scargill's garaged Rover, a new assistant Chief Constable who was in the SAS, and the gangs of fake miners, these are the rumours a war breeds. But the bitterness is real, and in its own way killing. The police, Healy says, are 'licking their wounds', while the South Yorkshire chief constable, Peter Wright, is a 'haggard man'. 'They're taking no notice of us councillors now, but as long as we remain in charge,' Healy continues –

with abolition of the South Yorkshire council closing in from Westminster – 'there are certain officers who will not get promoted.'

At the South Yorkshire council offices in Barnsley we meet the county police committee's Labour chairman, George Moores. 'I've been a right-wing socialist all my life,' he declares, but he is a red rag to the charging bulls in blue. Moores, in his mid-sixties, is himself an ex-miner and ex-Coldstream Guards sergeant with a Second World War wound, who once ran a pub next to the Rotherham police station. 'It was always full of them, sometimes [chuckling] at two or three in the morning.' He's called some of the police 'yobbos in uniform', as well as 'rosy-cheeked nice lads turned into Nazi storm-troopers', and says that he has been 'getting telephone threats in the middle of the night for it'. ('He opens his mouth in the wrong places,' said the buttoned-up police spokesman next day in Sheffield at the Snighill police head-quarters, on his best behaviour in a dove-grey suit, with matching tie and blue-grey moccasins; 'we look for support to elected leaders'.)

'I saw all I've worked for crash about my ears on 29 May when the horses charged at Orgreave,' Moores says. 'I'm a different police chairman from most,' he adds; 'the others are so damned idle. I must have been doing some good, because they gave me a bloody CBE for it.' Now he feels 'anguish, not anger' at the damage done to the 'very delicate balance between the police and the public'. Indeed, he claims to know that 'the videos of police aggression in South Yorkshire are going to be used as training manuals for a long time to come. They're going to start training policemen to be more belligerent in the future', including what he strangely calls 'intimidatory staring at a point in the centre of your forehead'. He calls it the 'end of an era' of 'community bobbying', of 'democratizing and humanizing the police force', and of 'policing by consent'. In fact, it was not so long ago, prior to the strike, that miners leaving the pits were joining the police themselves. But now it will be 'twenty years before some policemen in

South Yorkshire are forgiven for what they've done in the pit villages and on the picket lines'. Before the strike, 'we had an excellent force' and 'as good relationships as you could ask for'; the police were 'like pseudo-social workers' – 'we were proud of them, pride of possession if you like' – 'not banging on their shields like bloody Zulus'.

In a well-cut blue suit, with carefully brushed thick grey hair and upright in his bearing, Moores ('I could settle the strike tomorrow') describes himself as a 'disciplinarian at heart', who has 'always worked for, and with, the police in South Yorkshire. I'm an ex-Guardsman, a Britisher who served his country, and I say, if you step out of line, policeman or member of the public, you want hammering.' ('I'm a royalist, too, as well as a socialist,' he declares, and calls it – wrongly – 'a peculiar mix, I suppose.') Although they are 'weak, most of them' and 'emotionally unstable', he distinguishes between two different kinds of 'police leaders': 'those brought up the rough way through the ranks', and the 'academics', that is, the graduates, who have 'never fingered a bloody villain in their whole service'.

According to Moores, it is the former who have 'permitted themselves to become an arm of the government', and who are running the strike policing. He also claims that there has been a 'change in the character of the policeman. It is the older copper who says, "Calm it down, lads, calm it down." The younger ones are more arrogant, tougher. They get het up more quickly. And when they're away from their own patch', they turn into what he calls 'their own law-and-order people. But we're not paying yobbos to come into South Yorkshire to knock our own folk about, that's what I'm saying, when it's us, the community, who's got to clear up the bloody mess they've created'; a community, moreover, which has 'always taken pride in being lawful'. 'He's a union man,' they replied at police headquarters – baring their teeth and stepping well beyond the call of duty – 'looking for a nice safe seat when the county council is abolished.' 'He calls himself a right-wing socialist,' I said to the copper; 'I don't think we'd ever consider him right-wing,' was the police answer.

Moores alleges that 'some chief constables' – 'though they speak with forked tongues' – have told him that they're 'going to have a hell of a job getting these unruly young buggers back into normal policing. Anderton in Manchester is very considerably worried, so is Colin Sampson in West Yorkshire, and Philip Knights in the West Midlands. They're concerned because, when it's over, they'll have to take over a shambles.' And local policemen, 'some violently opposed to what is going on', have rung him throughout the dispute, saying, ' "We don't like it, you'll keep this to yourself, won't you, George, but we don't like it." In 1980, during the steel strike, some of these bobbies were at the demos outside Hadfield's, joining in the singing. Now they're having to arrest a lad for shouting "Scab!" who's done no bloody wrong in their eyes, and they say to me, "Who's he hurting?" I know many of them well. And I'll tell you there are some who don't like what these heavy-handed coppers in bloody riot-gear are doing, arresting people out coal-picking at tips, confiscating their bloody push-bikes and trumping-up charges against them. They phone me on the quiet, and say that if anybody other than a policeman had done what those coppers have been doing – like beating people into the ground at Orgreave – they'd have been charged immediately, and brought before the courts. They don't want anyone to know, and you'll never get to interview them' ('they've closed ranks, they won't speak'), 'because they'd be blacked by their colleagues. But they know I'll die before I reveal their names. They're carrying out orders, but they're being torn asunder' – he makes a strenuous manual gesture of rending – 'poor devils. What hurts the most is that they're having to do this to their own people.'

And who's to blame? According to Moores, the 'staring-eyed McLoughlin', for one, running the National Reporting Centre in London and co-ordinating police movements ('I don't like to see the image of the police go down because of him'); Labour MPs, who have 'sat on the fence so long, the iron has entered their souls'; and the Home Secretary, Leon

Brittan ('less than useless'), for another. He says that Brittan has personally warned him that 'all my threats and criticisms of the police have been noted down and documented. I don't know how to describe him,' says Moores, 'but if I did, I'd be accused of being a racist.' (This socialist and royalist ex-miner is many-sided.) 'There are too many of his ilk in parliament.' Ilk? 'It's worth looking at, that, even though there are some of them on our side. That shadow Home Secretary [Gerald Kaufman], for another, and he's not pulling any sods up, is he?'

As for the picketing, it had been 'a lark, war games for young stallions' – 'kids at heart, most of them, who can't stand still when they're talking to you, there's that much adrenalin running' – 'until people started being swayed by brutal thoughts', as the result of police action. 'There's nothing political about the lads on the picket lines,' he says confidentially. 'They're very sincere, but they don't know the difference between a Tory and a Labour MP, most of them.' ('They're not that stupid,' said John Healy, later.) ' "Maggie Thatcher" is only words, like "scab". The politics of it is nothing deep. It's all on the surface. It's about their right to earn a living. And what better achievement can any man have than drawing a wage?' he asked me.

On the road back from Barnsley to Doncaster – doomed to be a 'dole town' if the pits go under – the pit-heads are black across the dead winter fields, the sheep waiting in the rain for God-knows-what to happen. John Healy says that 'Where I work, at Carcroft Area mining workshops, many of them are Tory voters. They believe the mining industry is losing money and sections of it should be shut down. I say, "You're talking yourself out of a job", but they don't believe it. They don't think Labour has the answer. They're very much anti-union, they think the unions have too much power. If the rest of the movement doesn't help us, come the first anniversary of the strike in March, there could be a back-to-work situation.'

But there's no sign of it yet at Askern, outside Doncaster. Its huge Miners' Welfare is packed at 8 p.m. for an Old Folks'

Treat Night. The community is drawn in on itself, cocooned, stubborn, waiting. Three hundred yards away, all the windows and doors of the local police station are boarded up against assault. 'It's been attacked a few times,' say local strikers, without passion; 'the windows keep getting broken every time we replace them,' they say at Sheffield police headquarters. Two Askern police houses have also been attacked, one of them now boarded up and empty; a lone panda car (where once the bobby passed on his creaking cycle) speeds through the dreary and deserted village, breaking the limit. No policeman has been in the Miners' Welfare since the dispute started; and no one at the police station – though you can see the lights on through the narrow gaps in the boarding – answers my knocking. Nor, stretched along this ribbon road, is this really a 'village'; more a jerry-built, sodium-lit, suburban council-estate, or labour encampment.

The club secretary, Mike Porter, also on South Yorkshire county council, was arrested on his way to a picket at Babington colliery, despite being a member of the police authority. He says, his handshake soft as putty, that mining is 'like the sea. It's all we do. My dad was killed down the pit at thirty-nine; my uncle can't walk three yards with his lungs, and it took two grandads with pneumoconiosis. It's made me as I am; I had to be a man at ten, a fighter.' He has a beer belly, plump jowls, and 'A.M.W.' (Askern Miners' Welfare) embroidered over his left nipple. 'I showed 'em my county councillor's card. They said, "Are you going further?" I said, "Yes." They said, "You're going fucking nowhere." I said, "You must be fucking joking." "The only place you're fucking going, mate," they said, "is fucking Hucknall police station." They slammed me in one of those transporters, and took me to the bloody station. When I went in, this sarky bastard says, "Do we have to stand up for you then, Councillor Porter, seeing as how you're on the police committee?" "Do what you like," I told him. They searched me, fingerprinted me, and shoved me in a cell full of blood-and-shit-smears, filthy. I kept thinking, "Is this happening to me?" You had to bloody lick your spoon to eat the next lot,' he says, grimacing.

He has called for the chief constable's dismissal, and for his pains has had 'nine half-bricks' through *his* front-windows; 'they travelled the length of the room and hit the back wall. I'll never forgive or forget it.' He says, lip pursed with anger, that it's turned his eleven-year-old daughter 'into a wreck' – she was alone in the house at the time, screaming into the telephone to him, as the bricks came through the window – 'but I'll rebuild her'. He claims that working miners have their own 'hit-list', and that his name is on it. 'I've had letters from Nottingham, signed "beaten-up working miner", calling me a "big bastard", "anti-police", "anti-labour". After the bricking,' continues Porter, 'the lads here went berserk and bricked the four local scabs' houses. But when a man like me, a respectable community leader who's always been helpful with the police – I've even organized police dos in the Welfare, but all that's finished – when a man like me has lost confidence, has got contempt for what he's seen the police doing, what do you think the rest of the lads round here are thinking?' It is easily imagined. 'They're paying rates to help the police to beat 'em up, that's what they're thinking; to truncheon 'em, paying for horses to cavalry charge 'em. They're saying, "Me kids are cold, there's a heap of coal out there, it's a nationalized firm, and woe betide anyone who stops me." '

Porter thinks that the Coal Board plans to sell the Selby coalfield – and others – to ICI or the 'oil barons', and says he himself 'would steal to keep my kids, never mind being on the county council'. On the club-stage and in a warm glow, a local chanteuse in high heels and a swirl of petticoats is belting out 'You won't find another fool like me'. 'The electricity's been a right bastard,' says Porter, 'but there's no point the bloody building societies foreclosing on a thousand miners' houses.' Why not? 'Because they couldn't sell them.' Up the road, Porter continues, a local store was recently 'looted', 'wiped out'. 'It must have been the miners,' he says, 'the only things they left behind were t' bloody firelighters. There's no fear and there's no respect for the law in Askern; they've stole, and to survive they'll go on stealing. They've not got a lot going for them. Young lads without jobs in Askern are still in bed at 3 p.m., there's that little to get up for. But they're not yobbos. They know that if we give in, they've got no chance at all in this village.' He suddenly seems choked, or bewildered; and no wonder, with some fifty pits, and 50,000 miners in them, in the Yorkshire coalfield. 'From day one, bar the four scabs, it's been solid.'

The police themselves call Askern a 'trouble spot'. For a weekly outlay of £400–£500, the Miners' Welfare, 'with support from everywhere, including four thousand dollars just come in today from America', provides 350 'grown-ups and kids' with one meal a day, five days a week. 'They cut a few logs and find summat for themselves at weekend.' It costs two pence per raffle ticket for a £5 Dewhurst meat voucher. Many of the older men – old long before their time – are hard-breathing and pigeon-chested, walking with a gingerly step or coughing; some with close-cut Brylcreemed hair, Fair-Isle pullovers, flapping turn-ups and highly polished sturdy shoes. It's Yorkshire grit and bonhomie all right in here, but under severe duress. There's a death's-head rictus behind this welcome, in among the coughing. Outside, the pit looms in the dark, silent. Inside, there's singing. 'It'll take generations to put the pieces back together,' says Porter. 'The Yorkshire police are frightened to death of when the strike is over. They're telling the Met boys, "It's all right for you bastards, you won't have to police this area." They believe, and I believe, there'll be a revenge period.'

But if the police do think this, they aren't letting on next morning at Snighill, the multi-million-pound plate-glass and concrete palace which houses the South Yorkshire police headquarters in Sheffield. ('I'd get rid of it,' said George Moores. 'It's all bureaucracy, hundreds go in but nobody ever comes out.') 'The community bobbies are back in the villages already,' according to Sergeant Tom Walton, smart in civvies and uptight as a bedspring, 'there are no no-go areas in South Yorkshire.' And what about the hatred? 'When you get into a

police uniform,' says Walton tersely, his complexion a bit
florid and hectic for a man in his early thirties, 'you're
expected to be whiter than white – don't get me wrong, that
remark's not racist – and you have to put up with ridicule,
profanity and derogatory comments.' What do you call what
you're doing in South Yorkshire? 'Providing the means by
which miners can go to work uninjured.' But what about all
the police violence? 'It's a flexible style of policing, to deal
with every eventuality, responding. They try to test us, and
we respond to it. We could respond indefinitely.' The phone
keeps ringing. 'The trouble is', says Walton, reaching for the
receiver, 'that when we lose a battle, they shout, "Indians".'
'Not much,' he says into the phone to Chief Inspector Paget,
'except a fairly good rape at Hoyland.' He has a broad gold
band on his ring-finger. 'Eighteen-year-old, tied up and raped'
– a 'good rape', he again calls it – 'and robbery from a debt
collector, one hundred and nine pounds. Nothing much else,
sir,' he says riffling through his papers. He replaces the
receiver. I notice you use words like 'battle' and 'victory',
Sergeant. 'We don't use them,' he answers.

On the wall are specially printed blow-ups of excerpts from
speeches and interviews by Moores and Scargill. (For example, ' "I think everyone in the Nottingham coalfield would be
better employed coming out on strike," A. Scargill, Radio
Sheffield, 6.8.84.') 'But Scargill's lost his way with the
dispute,' declares Sergeant Walton, 'fighting the police.' But
what about the police themselves? Since when have they
defended the 'right to work', of tiny numbers at some pits,
with thousands of policemen and at a cost of tens of millions?
'We're getting men to work when they request an escort. It
was not the original intention to defend the right to work as
such.' Do the working miners want an escort of thousands?
'All but one or two do, like a lad at Kiveton, six foot eight
inches and built like a brick shit-house, who insists on going in
without us. That's his privilege, he has the right to walk in,
any way he wants, but both we and the NUM would prefer
him not to.' Do you see it as a pure issue of law and order, a

battle for democracy, or the class struggle? 'I'm not equipped to answer.' Aren't you fed up with the whole thing? 'We regret being dragged into a long drawn-out dispute, being the kicking post for most of them, instead of there being a negotiated settlement, which is right in any dispute.' So you're tired of taking the brunt of it? 'We're not taking the brunt of it. We're caught in the middle.' What do you want to see happen, then? 'We'd be grateful if there were a negotiated settlement.' But why have so few people in the police said that so far? 'Perhaps because nobody has asked us,' said Sergeant Walton, without expression.

At Treeton, a pit village high above Orgreave coking plant, the rain weeps on the ravaged tree-less landscape, melancholy beyond rescue. The tatty bungalows have been pitched down in bleak hillside crescents, insubstantial against the Pennine weather. It is a cold and thin world, pinched and gimcrack, of coal tips and the cliff-like escarpments and outworks of decades of coal-getting. Here, there is nothing to be born, or re-born; not a minefield trip-wired for explosion, but a burnt-out case, already gutted. From the upper deck of the bus, you can see the swastikas and NF signs painted on the roofs of the Treeton bus shelters and on the grey-yellow granite pillars of an abandoned railway-bridge. In the grocer's, windows bleared by rain, there are loud and difficult conversations, a desperate cheeriness trying to hold its own against the slow death of coal mining. Below the village, Orgreave is a black eyesore, a behemoth crouching in the devastated valley, gas-holders bulging in mountains of coke and black slurry.

'They need us more than we need them,' said the copper on the desk at Snighill, 'it'll soon come back to normal.' 'The police are tired after ten months,' said George Moores, 'they're finding it too much for them. I wish it was all over.' 'It's not going to be plain sailing, after,' said Sergeant Walton. 'We're praying for a terrible winter,' said John Healy. 'It's getting easier every day,' said Mike Porter at Askern. 'Scargill 'll disappear into oblivion after he loses this lot,' said the Doncaster Fone-A-Car taxi-driver – 'you hear bits of everything in this job. The police are not popular, but neither are the miners' – his takings £30 a week down, and himself an ex-miner whose uncle 'died down the pit at Hatfield. It's been a gamble that could have worked, but it hasn't. Scargill's played his long shot, and failed.' On 1 May 1891, four years before his death, Engels complained to August Bebel of the 'ill-advised strike of angry passion'; 'God have mercy on the poor strikers,' he added.

The Men of Harlech, and District

April 1985

'I'm prepared to say "bugger it". I've joined Plaid Cymru. The Labour Party', declares an angry English northern voice – pitching it a bit strong, or carried away by Welsh *hwyl* – 'has never done anything for the working class. They're a load of wankers, sending their kids to private schools, and can't wait for the fucking ermine.'

We are deep in Plaid Cymru country – the North Wales constituency of Meirionnydd Nant Conwy, in the new county of Gwynedd, where the Labour serpent, or Welsh Goliath, bit the dust in the 1983 general election, narrowly saving its deposit. The lounge bar of the Queen's Hotel, Harlech, is packed with beards, jeans, pints and anoraks, for a meeting of the left. Beyond the window, and the room's smoking anger – 'twenty per cent of the Welsh working class is bloody unemployed, and most of the rest of them are up to their arses in debt' – the deserted sands curve to the Atlantic estuary of the River Dwyryd, a white seagull flying in a cerulean sky. Neat, dapper, pink-cheeked in an olive-green corduroy suit, a green tweed cap on the bench beside him and a green scarf emblazoned with red Welsh dragon, Dafydd Elis Thomas, the thirty-eight-year-old president of Plaid Cymru and its local MP (AS, in Welsh), listens intently in the whorls of fag smoke.

Above us, the dark castle looms over these new men of Harlech. It was from here that Owen Glendower, or Owain Glyndwr, ruled his breakaway kingdom in the early years of the fifteenth century; a true Prince of Wales to the Welsh, and a 'Welsh rebel' – against Henry IV – to the English. 'Our analysis', Elis Thomas tells the crowd, 'must go beyond Labourism. Wales must be able to respond, in a coherent way, to its own economic crisis. And Welsh socialist democracy requires Plaid Cymru.'

In Meirionnydd and neighbouring Caernarfon, which Dafydd Wigley holds with an absolute majority of 11,000, Plaid Cymru, or the 'Party of Wales', founded in 1925 by preachers and teachers – 'a Welsh party', they'll tell you, 'not a Welsh nationalist party' – is a restored Adam in the Nonconformist paradise garden of what the English like to call Snowdonia, and which the Welsh now call Gwynedd. At its 1981 conference at Carmarthen, Plaid Cymru declared itself for a 'Welsh socialism', entering upon the very tilting-ground of Labour. And in November of the same year, the Plaid's 'National Left' was set up, a Welsh 'new left' movement: to 'unite all progressive elements in Wales', Plaid members or not, Welsh or English, and to 'promote the creation of a Welsh democratic state'. The smoke, eye-stinging, thickens.

'The Labour Party', says Elis Thomas, the avatar of the 'marginalized' Welsh – and here perceived as Glyndwr's political vicar on earth in the Palace of Westminster – 'is incorporated into the British state'; and, running full tilt on his frisky Welsh charger, 'dumb Labour MPs are delivered up by the valleys and by reactionary Welsh rugby supporters. Clapped-out Labourists', he continues, 'now constitute a permanent right-wing opposition in the House of Commons'; the Labour Party, with which he claims a 'love-hate relationship' – but whose whip he takes in the House of Commons – 'failed the Welsh miners' in a strike which wrought 'qualitative changes' in 'Welsh political awareness'; Britain, an heraldic dragon which must be slain in the regions, is 'in a state of reactionary crisis'.

Thomas, mercurial, is undismayed by the Welsh electorate's rejection of the last Labour government's modest devolution plans in the 1979 referendum. The answer for Wales, he says to the attentive crowd, is not 'ultra-leftism' ('useless'), not violent direct action ('you have to win people, there is no alternative to a democratic movement'), not 'separatism', not 'independence', not a 'depoliticized cultural politics', not 'Welsh-language Welshness in a vacuum', not even 'Welsh nationalism', pure and simple. (Then what the hell is it?) At this point, a black-bearded Welsh-speaking chauvinist in the crush beside me – later described to me as a 'Free Welsh Army type, an extreme right-winger, he'd frighten you' – shouted 'Bollocks!' in plain enough English, and left in a high Welsh dudgeon, slamming the bar-door behind him.

The 'way ahead' lies in a 'decentralized Welsh socialism', anti-Whitehall, GLC-inspired, and based on 'Welsh community consciousness'; a route – or is it the destination? – which is inscribed with the term 'workers' control in action'; and which means, *inter alia*, 'the Welsh people increasingly getting the experience of their own power, in those spaces where capitalism has foundered'. The price of not taking it is the further unabated 'ransacking' of the Welsh colonial economy by England. At the last general election, a significant number of local trade union branches in the constituency deserted the Labour Party. 'They voted for the progressive candidate,' says Dai Michael, the secretary of Meirionnydd trades council – who has himself left the Labour Party – 'and that wasn't Labour.' He describes Labour in Wales as 'almost totally corrupt', 'an empty machine'; 'when any people with ideas come into it, they get driven out again'.

On the road inland to Maentwrog and Tan-y-Bwlch, in the sheltered Vale of Ffestiniog – 80 per cent Welsh-speaking, and only a few Welsh miles, or *milltir*, from the rock of Harlech – a flock of hardy sheep browses in the rough pasture; with energetic crows, feathers blown by the wind and strutting near-sideways, keeping a sharp (community-conscious) look-out amid the droppings. Along the road, Welsh property rights are marked *preifat*, while *ar werth* signs placard the desirable bijou residences, put up for sale as the spring advances.

Steve Elliston, mine (genial English cockney) host at the Oakley Arms in Tan-y-Bwlch, is an ex-amateur pugilist, builder and landscape gardener, lover of Wales, and a semi-professional rough diamond, latterly from Dulwich. Slumped in chintz, another boxer – twelve years old and a dog – snores beside him. 'Some of them', says Elliston ('them' being the local Welsh), 'won't talk English at all, but some are very decent. It's like the whites and coloureds.' The old boxer stirs in its canine dream, or nightmare. Dr Who, alias Jon Pertwee, 'actually stayed' in this hotel, Elliston tells me.

Outside, in the lee of the winds, are dwarf oak-woods and rhododendron, and last year's underbrush of fern and bracken, in a tangle. Elsewhere in the grounds, he has 'cleared the old piggeries' and the overgrown tennis-court, and passionately felled trees as single-handedly as an Errol Flynn in the Burmese jungle. 'If you left it to the Welsh,' he says, a swollen bunch of fives – from fighting and hard labour – on the armrest beside me, 'you'd get nothing done. I don't know how anyone could be a Welsh nationalist; they couldn't support themselves for five minutes. It takes an Englishman to do anything round here,' he adds, chaffing the Welsh cook-and-waitress, or skivvy, Morwed ('it took me six bloody months to pronounce it'). 'They're unreliable, the Welsh.' 'You don't mean it,' she says. 'I do.' 'Okay, you don't have to knock it down,' says Morwed, game for a fight, her young teeth black with smoking, or carious. 'He's always making jokes about the Welsh,' she says to me, 'but he doesn't mean it.' 'Listen here,' Steve says, jabbing the air, 'I'm telling you, they're different.' (He may be serious.) 'A man'll come in here and spend every penny he's got.' So what? say I. 'If a Welshman's got ten pence left, he'll ask you to fill his glass up just by that much,' he says, holding out an almost-closed thumb and index finger. Morwed sighs, long-suffering. 'They won't take a jug, drinking,' he exclaims – gripping an invisible pint-jar in his fist – 'not them, they all want the straight glasses.' Banter or earnest, 'it's bloomin' true,' says Steve, in Cockney; 'oh no, it isn't,' says Morwed, in the rhythm of Gwynedd. 'And I always know when the customers are talking about me,' Steve says to me in an exaggerated whisper, winking. 'How?' asks Morwed, wide-eyed. 'They talk in Welsh,' he answers. 'Oh, they don't,' said Morwed, pretending.

'Some words', she says, innocently, 'I can't understand in English, not the big words.' 'She can't even swear in Welsh, she can't,' says Steve to me, pursuing his own quarry, or boxing southpaw, 'she has to use English. If you've got to use English words for swearing, it's not a complete language, is it?' he says to Morwed. Are you proud to be Welsh? I ask her. 'I don't know,' she replies, awkward. 'As long as she gets her cigarettes,' says Steve, teasing, 'she's happy.' 'Oh, you!' says Morwed. Not far from us, a Mickey Mouse world, fostered for the English tourist, beckons: the Englishman's Wales of pottery centres, icons of tall-hatted women at the loom and small-gauge railways; of antique shops and pony-trekking. The jobless in the area, 20 per cent and over, shadow every conversation. 'A man of thirty now,' says Steve, comfortable in his armchair, 'if he's done two years' work since he left school, he's done well here, he's done a lot.' (Morwed: 'It's not, it's all over the place, England.' Steve: 'How do you know?' Morwed: 'I've seen it on the telly.') 'Fortunately,' he adds, persistent, 'there's plenty of English about, plenty of plastering and building.' In the hills above us, beside Blaenau, above the purple-grey scree and Forestry Commission conifers, you'll even find the hideaway second homes of three of England's leading socialist historians. Around here, those in the know call it a 'second Hampstead' among the sheep-tracks.

Up in Blaenau, overhung with granite, its crags crowned by sunlight, the unemployed and tumbledown hillsides are a torrent of grey-black, blue-grey slate-stone. It was once the redoubt first of Liberals, then of Labour; though some, now, have their doubts about how solid it ever was for Labour. For the quarrymen of Blaenau were slow to accept Labour candidates; even in 1945 it was the Liberals who won Meirionnydd. But in February 1974, when the Meirionnydd constituency first fell to Plaid Cymru, with a 588 majority over Labour, few could have foreseen the decade of Labour's political decline which was then to follow.

Elwyn ('I was one of the 588') Griffiths is a fifty-four-year-old social worker, and member of Plaid Cymru. His father, a small farmer and quarryman in Blaenau, 'was Labour, voted Labour to the end of his life, but as Plaid Cymru is today

would have voted for it'. How is Plaid Cymru today? 'Socialist, unlike Labour.' And what is Labour? 'A party with
imperialist attitudes towards what it sees as small nations, and
small people.' His father, he says, 'couldn't speak English, or
only broken English', and, born in the 1880s, 'belonged to a
nineteenth-century anti-English tradition'. Anti-English?
'When I say "anti-English", I put it in a crude way. It was,
rather, a bundle, or cluster, of beliefs. My father was against
English influence, but on good terms with individual English
people. I have this myself,' Griffiths adds, 'in a watered-down
version.' He also has a copy of the *New Statesman* sticking out
of his pocket.

According to Griffiths, who voted Labour until 1974 (and
was educated like Dafydd Wigley at Manchester University, as
an adult student), Labour's decline in the area – 'it's been the
real shaking up of the political monkey-puzzle' – was 'pro-
voked by the new breed of Welsh Labour MPs sent to
parliament in 1966. Though graduates of Welsh universities,
they did not do what we expected of them.' And Neil Kinnock
of Bedwellty and the University of Cardiff, who led the 1979
Welsh Labour Party campaign *against* devolution? 'I wouldn't
trust him to feed the chickens,' Griffiths says; his role, as an
'opportunist Welsh boyo', is not forgiven. The gradual transformation of Plaid Cymru from a 'mere cultural pressure
group' to a 'political movement on the left, incorporating local
ILP and Welsh Nonconformist chapel traditions' has been the
consequence of these defeated expectations.

'Labour had a vision once,' Griffiths continues, his sleeves
patched with leather and his socks yellow; 'Keir Hardie and all
that,' he calls it. (In fact, Keir Hardie – 'one of the visionaries
I'd always relate to,' says Griffiths – was first elected to
parliament from Merthyr.) 'But they jumped on the gravy
train, especially in Wales, seeing it as merely an electoral
reserve to be exploited,' and are 'prepared to sacrifice absolutely everything, including the miners, to gain office. Kinnock's Britain would not be significantly different from
Thatcher's. For us, Labour has come to the end of its historic

purpose,' even if 'old Labour people' have to 'drag themselves away from their loyalties and vote in the night for Plaid Cymru'. And what of Plaid Cymru's nationalism? 'The word in Welsh, *cenedlaetholdeb*, doesn't conjure up your kind [my kind?] of jingoism and flag-waving. In England, it can mean Ascot races, Changing of the Guard, any bloody thing. In Welsh, it suggests community, being together.'

Or did, in this district where there are now hardly any miners or quarry workers to sustain it. ('We had our recession a long time ago,' say the town's voices, 'it's the rest of Wales that has caught up with us.') Many of Blaenau's chapels – more tabernacles than chapels – the three cinemas, two of the three billiard halls and the dance hall are closed; though the Jerusalem Independent Chapel is still in business. The wind soughs through the abandoned quarry buildings, roofless and eyeless. On a wall, the Free Wales Army (with its symbol a near-swastika), from which Plaid Cymru keeps a determined political distance, has signed the word CYMRU; rivulets of whitewash are frozen on the harsh grey granite.

A half-mile away, off Blaenau's High Street, you can find the focus of dismay and disillusionment among local ex-Labour converts to Plaid Cymru: Owen Edwards, town councillor, district councillor, JP, chairman of a bench, school governor, member of the trades council, delegate to the Gwynedd association of trades councils, member of the community health council and the Gwynedd joint consultative economic committee, secretary of the Gwynedd magistrates' association and secretary of the Meirionnydd constituency Labour Party ('I wonder if I can remember something else'), Labour's Pooh-Bah and panjandrum.

'I've been', he says, 'a great admirer of Lloyd George all my life. He was the big man here, he's my main political hero.' On Edwards's bookshelves are biographies of Ramsay MacDonald and Neville Chamberlain; *The Speeches of Lord Birkenhead*, a Cobbett and a Winston Churchill; a *Dictionary of Synonyms*, the Bible, *Home Decorating and Repairs* and *The World's Greatest Wonders*. A pot statue of Dick Turpin stands in the fireplace. A retired headmaster and 'Calvinistic Methodist' ('my grandmother was a great chapel woman'), Edwards was born in Porthmadoc of 'non-political' parents. His 'chapel background' – 'though now I'm closer to the Bishop of Durham' – has given him, he says, a 'moral attitude to poverty, fair play, and all the rest of it'. He has small, deep-set eyes and a brisk moustache; and spent the war on the RAF ground staff, mostly at Stradishall in Northern Ireland. 'I nearly lost my life,' he added, 'when the Germans came to bomb there.' He claims that 'the Nash' – the pejorative term for Plaid Cymru – 'have had their knives in me for a long time'. But he is also regarded as the broker of Labour's local political downfall.

'He's been the death of the Labour Party in Meirionnydd,' says Dafydd Elis Thomas; 'he's been at the helm,' says Rob Humphreys, son of a small farmer from Llanymynech and the Labour Party's disaffected former agent in the neighbouring (Liberal-held) seat of Montgomery, 'while Labour has been going under. He's charted Labour's decline in north and mid-Wales, and just can't see it.' In the town, he is jokingly (or not so jokingly) accused of advising Labour Party supporters at the last election to vote Tory, in order to keep out the leftists of Plaid Cymru. 'I can get on with the Tories and Liberals in Blaenau,' he says himself, 'we have a good laugh together, but not Plaid Cymru. They won't look at me.' 'We pass them in the streets,' says Plaid's Elwyn Griffiths about Labour, 'there's no relationship between us.' Owen Edwards described Griffiths in turn as a 'nut-case, with a house full of hippies'.

On the Wales executive of the Labour Party for years, and the teller who – tripping over the numbers – announced the Kinnock leadership victory to the 1983 Labour Party conference, Edwards deals out hard and direct judgments, quick eye (in half-moon specs) darting: upon Labour's 'left' and 'leftish' ('all permanent opposition') types; upon the 'divisive Nash' ('they have an inferiority complex, that's why they blame the English for this, that and the other'); upon Dafydd Elis

Thomas ('a well-known Marxist, whose socialism scares his supporters'); upon CND ('and all that stuff'), and what he calls 'Greenham Common-type women' ('you can't blame the local people, with all the sanitation problems, the mess, and lying down in front of the traffic'); and upon 'gay groups, black groups, anti-fishing and anti-hunting groups, and all the rest of it in the Labour Party'.

A tit is picking at a pink salami-shaped net of nuts beyond his patio windows; a commemorative 1969 royal investiture chair ('a silly Ruritanian exercise', Dafydd Elis Thomas had called it), its head-rest carved with the Prince of Wales's heraldic feathers, stands in state on his lounge carpet. How would you describe yourself? I ask him. 'I was Kinnock's right-hand man in North Wales in the campaign against devolution. I'm a Kinnock-and-Hattersley supporter,' he answers. What is that? 'Neither left nor right.' What then? 'I'm a common-sense, practical, realistic socialist, who wants to see the Labour Party back in power. Politics without power is useless.' In 1983, Labour won twenty – and the Tories advanced to fourteen – of Wales's thirty-eight parliamentary seats, with 37·6 per cent of the popular vote. In 1966, Labour had held thirty-two out of the thirty-six seats – and the Tories three – with 60·6 per cent of the voters. How will power be won again? 'By trimming our sails to what the people want, to the aspirations of the electorate, Orpington-type aspirations, with their mortgages, fridges, colour TVs, and all the rest of it.' 'The hard coalface of Welsh political realities', at which the Plaid Cymru men, sleeves rolled up, usually claim to be working, obviously means something different to Edwards.

'And let me tell you this,' he continues. 'If you're political round here, you get a hell of a lot of umbrage. In a rural constituency like Meirionnydd, very few people have strong political views. You're in a non-political area. The box decides it. The box is the political centre of all things. Once, in Blaenau, you'd have three to four hundred at meetings for Aneurin Bevan, Barbara Castle or Anthony Greenwood. Now you're lucky to get half a dozen.' He gazes out briefly on to his patio, his pencil-thin moustache as neatly trimmed as need to be the sails of Labour. 'Frankly speaking, there are very few people left in Wales on the poverty line. Poverty traps are minimal now, compared to the 1930s. In pockets, yes; there are some who can't heat their homes even here in Blaenau.' ('I'm fortunate,' he added, 'I've got two pensions.') 'Now you get all these Labour Party supporters saying to you, "Mrs Thatcher has got some good points, Owen." They're all miniature little Conservatives, whoever they vote for.' In Meirionnydd, the Tories, with 28·5 per cent of the poll in 1983, came a strong second to Plaid Cymru. 'The Nash', he declares, expressionless, 'are no long-term threat to Labour. For some of them,' he says with destructive shrewdness, 'culture is the main plank' – 'language before people', he calls it – 'for others, devolution. You don't know exactly what they do want.' And true enough, Labour's steady decline in Wales from 1966 to 1983 has been matched by Plaid's electoral decline during the same period. With 7·6 per cent of the total Welsh poll, and a grand total of two members elected, it was Plaid Cymru's lowest vote since 1970. But, I ask him, isn't it now attracting increasing radical support?

'First of all,' he answers, 'the only true radical party in Wales is the Labour Party. Second, there is no economic foundation for a free Wales, Welsh embassies abroad, devolution, Welsh language, or whatnot. With forty-eight million English people paying rates and taxes, we can always call on the English to subsidize our deficiencies. Third, two-thirds of the Welsh population live in South Wales, in the valleys, not here. Most of them are English-speaking only, solid Labour. But if the Labour Party sticks to unilateral nuclear disarmament, the Tories will beat them.'

Around the corner, Labour councillor Arthur Holland-Williams, a Gas Board service engineer in a plaid shirt and black pullover – accused by Edwards of 'having one foot in the camp of Labour, and one foot in the camp of Plaid Cymru', at which he laughed uproariously, throwing himself back on the sofa – has Tony Benn's *Arguments for Democracy* and a current copy of *Tribune* on his front-room table. 'Our values are totally different,' says Williams of Edwards, 'we are from totally different wings of the party. And some would say,' he adds drily, word by word, 'that Owen Edwards has one foot in the camp of Labour, and one foot in the camp of the Tory Party.' He is intense and dark-eyed, thin (or gaunt) and with greying hair; his father, a quarry labourer ('I'm told that he was a very hard worker') went out to Canada in 1912 as a boy, 'working on locos' as a coppersmith and steam-fitter. 'Even when he was fifteen or sixteen,' Williams declares, 'we can see from his letters home that he was a convinced Marxist.' He returned to work in the Blaenau quarries, and to become one of the local CP's founder-members.

'In those days,' Williams continues, sitting forward, 'my father would say that they used to have such great discussions in the quarry. Each morning, he would buy two copies of the *Daily Worker* from the newsagent: one for himself, and one to put in the public library in Blaenau.' He speaks with delibera-tion; as of a man translating Welsh thoughts (and strong feelings, or obsessions) into a careful English. 'Today,' he says, 'many people of a socialist persuasion have been attracted to Dafydd Elis Thomas.' Are Labour activists leaving to join Plaid Cymru? 'Many would not want to be divorced from the party. But it has happened, and it is happening.' Why? 'Because Plaid Cymru is the vanguard party promoting social-ism in Meirionnydd. And Dafydd' – 'the greatest politician Wales has ever seen' – 'with his vision, is bringing Welsh radicals together. Party labels are being transcended. It is a trend I would like to see being established more widely.' You mean, in Wales? 'More widely. And if I have to choose between someone who has a Labour Party label and a true socialist, I would choose a socialist always.'

But isn't Plaid Cymru, whatever it may say of itself, nationalist before it is socialist? He carefully composes his answer. 'Oh, no. But even if it was, language and culture' – to which I hadn't myself referrred – 'are very, very important.

What', asks the service engineer for the Gas Board, 'are we doing when we use language?' Outside, you can hear children shouting indistinctly. Inside, the unlived-in and cold front room is silent. 'We are expressing our experience.' He stares at me intently; yet Elwyn Griffiths, the Plaid member, had himself described 'the Welsh language issue' as a 'bloody hindrance, when it gets emotive'. 'And one type of experience can be best explained in one language,' Williams continues, speaking slowly, 'and another in another. Welsh language and culture, a culture that does not divide but enriches, are in danger.' The percentage of Welsh speakers in Meirionnydd fell from 73·5 per cent in 1971 to 67·9 per cent ten years later; it even plummeted from 87 to 85 per cent in Blaenau. 'If the Welsh language died, it would be a great loss to humanity, to lose such an expression of experience. I would be just as strongly in favour of protecting the English language, I would do everything in my power to protect it, if it was dying,' he says, his gimlet eyes shining.

Back down on the ground in Penrhyndeudraeth – where Bertrand Russell used to live, and over 80 per cent are Welsh speakers, a proportion which is rising – Jim ('I'm Anglo-Welsh') Wallington has an English mother, a 'Welsh-speaking British' father (a lorry driver who votes Tory, whom his son describes as a 'very integrated Welshman', and who regards Plaid Cymru as 'crackpot'), a Dublin Irish wife, and two young bilingual daughters. A former motorway labourer, barman and record-shop assistant, he is now a mature student at Coleg Harlech. 'We didn't speak Welsh at home at all. To all intents and purposes', he says, 'I was brought up as English in an English working-class home.' What do you mean? 'The *Daily Mirror* and all that.' It was the 1969 investiture of Prince Charles as Prince of Wales, at nearby Caernarfon, which turned him towards Plaid Cymru. 'In the streets round here at the time', Wallington continues, 'there were a lot of large men walking about, plain-clothes Special Branch. If there was a knot of you outside the pub talking, they sent you on your way. We were supposed to be plotting.' Plotting what? 'To plant bombs at the castle. A few of my friends were set up, and lifted.'

Seven years a Plaid member, he is more sceptical than most about Plaid's future: 'All we got in 1980 and 1983 was lost deposits, lost deposits. You can't go on like that.' Moreover, there is an 'ideological crisis in the party', between the 'petit-bourgeois anti-left culturalists, for whom Scargill is a dirty word' and who 'can't see any connection between Plaid Cymru and the miners' struggle' – some of the members of his party branch are 'almost fascist in outlook' – and the 'Gramscian socialists' around Dafydd Elis Thomas. The latter's talk about 'English hegemony' and 'subaltern peoples' (the contribution to Plaid Cymru of its leading guru, Professor Gwyn Williams) 'is scaring the life out of them. There is a danger of leaving people behind with that stuff. But I keep asking myself, "Am I bringing things down to too simple a level?" '

On his own bookshelves in the tiny terrace cottage, facing the washed-out grey-green water-meadows, are Raymond Williams's *The Long Revolution*, Robert Oakeshott's *The Case for Workers' Cooperatives*, Kenneth O. Morgan's *Wales, 1880–1980*, and *Miners Against Fascism*. On the walls hang a framed robin, snowscapes and a windmill. 'I'd like to see a lot of Labour people down south in the industrial valleys coming over. But it seems to me they can be kicked in the teeth as often as you like, and they'll still come out and vote Labour.' The key, for him, is 'political education', or 'grass-roots politicization'; converting his own father, who says that 'we'd all be eating dirt, if the Welsh Nats had their way', would be a modest beginning. Owain Glyndwr, at least, managed to invade South Wales – by the non-parliamentary route to Welsh power – and to baffle the English armies; taking not only Carmarthen but Newport, and (by 1404) even Cardiff. But he lost more than his deposit in South Wales four years later, and by 1415 had been ignominiously 'readmitted to the English King's grace and obedience', for all the world as if Plaid Cymru were to be incorporated into the Welsh Labour Party.

'It was a harrowing experience,' says Iscoed Williams, Plaid Cymru's local constituency party chairman, of the 1979 referendum defeat of the devolution proposals, 'even though it was only the crumbs falling off Whitehall's table that we were offered.' The coal-flame leaps and flickers in his front room in Trawsfynydd as the day darkens, the grandfather clock ticking behind him. 'Oh heck,' he says, drawing in his pursed breath, and translating himself into unidiomatic English, 'how the guts were drained out of those who worked for it.'

A veteran Christian socialist ('the true-thinking Welshman abhors Toryism really'), he is the son of a stonemason who was 'a countryman at heart', 'kept alive the rural way of thinking', and who in 1934 joined Plaid Cymru. 'My father was a *Daily Herald* man. He saw no contradiction between being a socialist and being Plaid Cymru, and I see none either.' To Iscoed, ex-Bevin boy ('I had more of a fancy for the sea'), joiner, builder, WEA man and Baptist, Wales is a 'desolate wilderness'; 'one of the small, exploited and peripheral nations, which is treated merely as part and parcel of an English-based system'. (Gramsci's Sardinian shadow falls across our path even in Free Church Trawsfynydd.) 'But since the late 1960s,' he thinks, 'the English have begun to realize that beyond Offa's Dyke there is a people living.' He speaks with the gift of (two) tongues, of 'the decline that has come into the Welsh Labour Party' – 'it will never revive in North Wales, but in England it's got to' – as if it were one of the plagues of Egypt, or God's retribution for the politically unrighteous. And even if the Welsh are 'not enough politically minded' – 'they can't recognize what the political is, they can't comprehend a political statement,' he says finely – 'Plaid Cymru, with its brain capability, its way of thinking, and its leader, has the ability to be a Welsh political power'; ready and waiting, sword (and Bible) in hand, to deliver the unwilling Welsh from English thraldom.

'We have a leader,' he repeats, white-haired and fingers to his temples, 'and Dafydd Elis Thomas is the one. He can absorb all things, a brilliant mind, everything hanging on a peg, he can use it and enlighten the people. They say he is "left of this" and "left of that". But,' Iscoed declares, sitting by the fireside, 'you must remember where he came from, what was his father. His father was a Methodist minister of religion, a member of the ILP, from a quarrying background in Blaenau. It is a background which has proved itself. It is a background which would not lead you into destruction. They compare him with Englishmen, with Tony Benn, but they've got no business to do it.' Why not? 'Because you cannot compare a Welsh Plaid Cymru leader with something based on the English Labour Party. Welsh politics is different, because we have our own radicalism in Wales, because the whole background is different.'

How are they different? There is a silence, of musing in the fading firelight. 'An ordinary Englishman and an ordinary Welshman are two human beings. But I think there is something different between us. But if you ask me to explain what it is, I'd be in quite a quandary. You can see', he says in growing darkness, 'the difference, it's quite massive, it's there in front of you, but how do you put your finger on it?' There is a further silence, the clock ticking; three pot dogs stand on the mantel above us, two red and one black. 'Most of the difference', he says at last, 'is the language. You cannot translate feelings. Every question you have asked me, I have had to translate my answer from Welsh into English.' Dark and light fitfully chase each other. 'It could be a barrier,' he adds (is he earnest, or anxious, or inwardly smiling?), 'this discussion between us.'

I can hardly see him. 'Welsh has to be guarded, or the Welsh people is lost,' he continues, asking and answering his own questions. 'But we must also be a bilingual nation. We cannot permit language to be a political barrier among the Welsh people.' (Indeed, there are many non-Welsh-speaking Welshmen who resent what they see as the growing influence, in north and mid-Wales, of a Welsh language élite, or Mafia.) 'We have been tied to England for centuries, but there is also no point in breaking with England. Our dream', he says into the darkness, 'is of Plaid Cymru ruling the whole of Wales, with a Welsh government in a Welsh nation. It will be to the English benefit when we have a right to govern. At the moment, we are kept on the periphery, dormant. Wales, the Welsh nation of people, is politically drowsy, Wales is sleeping.' (Also, 'we have one eye closed and the other eye half-open'.) 'But one day revolution will come' – 'I don't mean a Bolshevik revolution, or anything of the kind' – 'when the ordinary Welsh people in the valleys rise up and say, "We've had enough." ' He gets up to poke the fire. 'We have to stand and say,' he says, poker in hand, ' "with Wales, thus far and no further".'

But for Emyr Williams, the young chairman of Plaid Cymru's National Left, a Gramsci-inspired student and son of a sheep-farmer, the first problem is that 'traditional Welsh history has been so mind-numbing'. The cat licks itself on the carpet beside him; we are in the small family-cottage, high up in Aberhosan, facing Plynlimon. 'It contains a particular definition of Welshness,' he says with distaste – 'historicist', he calls it – 'which focuses on a rural Wales, a romantic Wales, the "wild Wales" of George Borrow.' His father is sitting by the cottage door, his wellingtons set neatly on the floor beside him. 'It leads', Williams continues, 'to a backward, chauvinist, isolationist and idealist view of the future. Wales, at this conjuncture in its decline, and standing on the periphery of a periphery [sc. England], will not reproduce itself on such a basis.' 'The wind keeps poking under the door,' says his father, apologizing.

'To rebuild', declares Emyr Williams, 'we have a long way to go. But to achieve it [fists suddenly clenched], we must convert the radical perspectives of the Welsh people to a future-oriented vision.' What do you mean? He tries to come down from theory to practice, brow furrowed, the cat standing up and stretching. 'We must recognize the reality of the Welsh economic situation. We must reflect in Plaid Cymru the real aspirations of the Welsh people.' What are they? He pauses; 'That the marginalization of the Welsh economy, the plight of the small farming communities, the destruction of the valleys, be seriously tackled.' How? 'It's going to be a long, slow process addressing these problems, not simply a matter of nationalization of this or that' – 'if you conceive of progress in those terms, you'll be in real trouble' – 'nor of "class analysis" and "class struggle".' What then? 'It is in the actual effort to do something about Welsh industrial decline that Welsh identity emerges. But we will have to move pragmatically, step by step, arousing popular consciousness in Wales of all the forces which are undermining our country.' Outside, the patient sheep stand against the wind in the shelter of stone walls, and boulders. To what end? 'To secure the establishment of a Welsh state.' To what end? He hesitates for a moment. 'So that working people can control in Wales their own means of production.' On the family bookshelf stand *Y Beibl*, Gorky's *My Childhood*, and Novello's pocket edition of Mendelssohn's *Elijah*.

Below Aberhosan, at Machynlleth, on the Montgomery and Liberal side of the frontier with Meirionnydd, Dafydd Elis Thomas is in town for a meeting (at the Owain Glyndwr Institute), and nineteen people – not many of them Gramscians – have turned out to hear him. Now 20 per cent unemployed, Machynlleth was called by George Borrow in 1867 a 'thoroughly Welsh town'. Today, only half of the inhabitants are Welsh-speaking, and the proportion is falling. Once upon a time, in 1402, Glyndwr was crowned in Machynlleth; even today you get your wholemeal and muesli at the *Cyfan Fwyd* shop, and your stamps at the *Swyddfa' R Post*, while the town's cop-shop and toilet finger-posts, 583 years on, point to the *Heddlu* in one direction, and the *Toiledau* in the other.

Elis Thomas speaks quietly and eagerly, in both Welsh and English, of 'minority nationalities who don't have states'; of Christianity as 'internationalist' and 'able to help us break out of this mentality of blocs'; of Plaid's 'politics of alliance', which has brought close involvement with the South Wales NUM, the women's movement, the green movement, and

CND. When he speaks in Welsh, I can understand only 'Heseltine', 'Greenham', 'Molesworth', and 'consensus'. In English, he describes the SDP as 'Fabians detached from the Labour Party' who would 'fail to deliver in Wales', but instead 'pour all their money into Basildon, if they were to come to power'; and assails Labour, as ever, for its 'top-down, central-ist thinking'.

A member of the audience plangently declares that 'we should back South Yorkshire, they're more independent than we are'. Thomas answers that 'regional and sub-national political and economic pressures are gradually intensifying, throughout Britain, to renegotiate relations with London'. Facing him, on the Institute wall – and facing Plaid's chosen route to trying to become a 'national popular movement' behind the backs of Labour – is a monumental stone plaque of Glyndwr, sword-wielding and in stone chain-mail, stone standards flying stiffly around him. Indeed, the trouble in Wales is not only that there are Welsh patriots in all the parties; but that many members of, and voters for, Plaid Cymru are conservatives and liberals, not socialists, and their radicalism (allegedly) 'petit-bourgeois'; that Plaid Cymru's 'socialism' is seeking to hold its own in agricultural constituen-cies and among small farmers; that the Welsh working class is much more strongly pro-Labour than is the English; and that the Welsh Labour Party is itself seen by many as the national party of Welsh working people.

'However, what concerns me', said Dafydd Elis Thomas, in his untidy room at the House of Commons, 'is the deepening and broadening of Welsh left culture. It's not the destruction or transformation of the Labour Party. For if it were to turn itself into a socialist party, we would all be part of that one big movement.' But Welsh Labour is 'doing the job it knows best: stifling radical ideas, rubbishing local initiative and suffocat-ing social protest'.

Regarded in his own constituency as a most comely man of 'vision' – 'they are not my visions, but a whole way of thinking' – he nevertheless disclaims 'everything to do with mystical

Wales in moonlight, at the top of Cader Idris. That sort of thing is out,' he says flatly, 'we've had enough of it.' Yet in his lapel he wears the Welsh CND badge, with its added yellow daffodil, for imagination; and declares, *en passant*, that the 'sound of Welsh singing brought tears to my eyes at a miners' rally'. Moreover, 'Welsh language, Welsh culture and Welsh nonconformity have given us an alternative system of values and education, a whole set of alternative communal ways of thinking to Labour's incorporation in the British state. It is on that basis that we can resist what the British state is doing to us.' ('The Welsh themselves may be diverse,' he added, 'but living in a peripheral economy is their common condition.') He describes the politics he espouses as 'a combination of class politics, the "new politics" of the late 1960s, and the cultural politics of Wales. We are not trying' – *pace* Iscoed Williams, his own constituency chairman – 'to create a nineteenth-century Welsh nation-state. Rather, we're trying, from Wales, to help in the transformation of the British state, trying to change a state which is an increasing threat to all our civil liberties, in alliance with progressive political forces' – 'the better forces', he calls them – 'in Britain.' The older, eurhythmic Welsh slogan-demand of *Iaith a Gwaith*, Language and Work, is not enough for Elis Thomas. 'The stage we are at', he says, 'is linking ourselves to Welsh socialist and especially ILP traditions, and pushing forward the notion that the Welsh people' – 'they're all the people who live on our side of the Severn' – 'must take control of their own affairs in the community and the workplace, must take power at the community level.' Earlier, in Trawsfynydd, I had asked Iscoed Williams what all the talk of a 'Gramscian strategy' for the Plaid Cymru signified to him. 'I have read a bit,' he had replied, beside the fire, 'thought a bit, but I am no scholar. To me, it means that Dafydd is trying to break into the circle where people discuss the price of cows in the market, the TV programme, or the preacher's sermon.' It was a good answer.

But to 'bury the Welsh Labour Party, and give it a quick state funeral', as Plaid Cymru's ideologue Gwyn Williams has brashly put it, is beyond the reach of these political undertakers. (Plaid itself has been described, in the *British Journal of Political Science*, as a 'dwarf plant which is sturdy, but cannot grow'.) Nevertheless, the struggle in North Wales with Labour for 'grass-roots', 'radical' support – or nonconformist souls – is an intense one. And though Plaid Cymru's policy of 'working for Welshness', within or without the British state, has as many faces as the town-clock in Tredegar, Labour's own time looks as if it may have come, and gone, in Meirionnydd.

On the Mersey Waterfront

November 1985

In this plague city – 'one of the most democratic in the country', according to the council's deputy leader, Derek Hatton – 'a boil on the arse of the Labour Party' is the least hostile of the local epithets for Militant. More a 'totalitarian regime' and a 'regime of terror' (Sir Trevor Jones, ship's chandler and Liberal leader); or a 'cancer in the bowels' (John Livingston, chairman of the dissident Vauxhall Ward Labour Party); a cancer which 'one has to cut deeply to have any chance of saving the body', according to John Jones, owner of the Continental Club and one of the organizers, with car salesman Jeff Tinnion, of Liverpool Against Militant, and of its October 1985 pier-head rallies of irate ratepayers.

But then even Ken Dodd of Knotty Ash was described to me as a 'well-known fascist' by a fast-talking, or feverish, lad in shirt-sleeves – with a smooth, executive haircut – in the town hall's Militant-organized 'Central Support [or propaganda] Unit'; 'I never realized I was such a confrontationist as I'm turning out to be,' he added. Trotsky's Transitional Programme has even 'raped the city', according to charity worker Joan Junkers (who runs an organization called 'Victims of Violence'). Worse still, as reports of the Militant contagion spread through the national night-club circuit, Bobby Shack, a popular local stand-up comic, has started telling his punters – in the spotlit darkness – that 'people in other parts of the country are actually frightened of us. If you meet Londoners,' he says, 'they don't want to know you.' And he doesn't seem to be joking.

Certainly, there's no mellow fruitfulness here in late autumn, not here on the hustling and hooligan waterfront of the River Mersey, where words themselves are used like knuckledusters. The threatened council workforce is a 'battering ram', or 'bulldozer', in the battle with Whitehall; Derek

Hatton is 'Militant's first megastar'; and every next person, according to Militant's strutting cocks o' the walk, combs bristling, is a 'Poujadist', 'coward', 'Freemason', 'right-wing careerist', 'petit-bourgeois traitor', or, perhaps worst of all, 'intellectual'. 'Workerism is the order of the day with Derek,' said Eddie Bannon, ex-Ruskin and a local trade union official. 'If you've got two O levels and can spell "bourgeois", Hatton'll think you want watching.'

But no wonder there's every kind of political suspicion and anger in a city with 25 per cent unemployment (70 to 80 per cent in Vauxhall, the ward that includes Scotland Road, and 90 per cent among young people in some districts); 65,000 jobs – 40,000 of them in manufacturing – lost in six years; 56,000 Liverpool households on supplementary benefit; 50,000 council tenants, together with half of Liverpool's domestic ratepayers, poor enough to receive rent or rate rebates; 22,000 on the council housing waiting-list; and the population (now half a million) down by a third in only two decades of steep decline. Balancing – or cooking – the books, with or without the help of Swiss bankers, can touch little of it.

From some jaundiced angles amid the ruined terraces and the tandoori parlours, with their flock, or fur, wallpapers, even the city's two cathedrals seem to be squaring up to each other: the gloomy pile of the darkened and deserted Church of England, louring over the last brass-plates of a lost merchant era, and Irish Catholicism's whited (or jerry-built) sepulchre, with its spiky, hollow corona. Local football, religiously followed – with *its* terraces the stamping-ground of the plebeian – is, or was, an alternative solace. Bill Shankly, former Liverpool manager, even used to call it 'socialism without politics'; though Trotsky himself, writing in 1925, thought football responsible in Britain (with boxing and racing) for 'drawing off working-class fervour into artificial channels'. But round here, with rising unemployment and shrinking resources, the artificial channels themselves seem to be contracting; with gate numbers fallen, a spate of own goals

– including those scored at the Heysel stadium – and one home defeat after another.

And in these coils of desperation (with unemployment 'corrosive' and a 'poisoned atmosphere in the city') no wonder, too, that local Labour is so belaboured; that so many short-haired entryists, beyond removal by the party's perspiring mole-catchers, should be burrowing and boring their way into Liverpool's political earthworks; and that the whole self-lacerating city has been scratching itself into a red inflammation, with the salve of jobs and renewal nowhere on the battered horizon. Instead, 'not doing the Tories' dirty work for them' – to compensate for cruel £350 million grant cuts since 1979 – has for months served to justify the 'impossibilist' principle of 'no rent and rate increases, no cuts in services and programmes, and no job losses', the scouse equivalent of Custer's Last Stand. In the ensuing shambles, over creamy pints of Guinness with heads as thick as pie-crusts, one man's 'Trotskyite bloody claptrap' – or 'touch of the Brownshirts' – has become another's red-blooded ardour in promotion of 'working-class interests' and Labour Party conference decisions; or a dead-eyed and driven sectarianism, doing its (and the Revolutionary Socialist League's) dour political duty.

At any rate, they talk tough and hard, these political scousers, feet on the brass rails of a thousand public houses; in a city which the Liverpool MP, Eric Heffer (crumpled and cantankerous in the Commons tea room), calls 'a very Celtic city, semi-anarchic in that sense, an independent city, a very working-class city'. Some, heads lowered to butt their opponents, are mere political boot-boys – not tribunes of the people – with fists stuck in the empty till of municipal socialism and names on the books of the Merseyside Fraud Squad. Others, dodging and weaving, have sought to defy the laws of economic gravity and the 1982 Local Government Act together, in the belief that 'when the issues are put clear to people, they will always vote for us', as the city economy collapses.

But behind the 'rough' Irish politics of the crowded

working-class shebeens and the Militant-manipulated trade union and Labour Party branches, which legitimates all this, are larger questions: of a hard-punching, lumpen street-'Trotskyism', breathless with authoritarian political excitement, and which is no more than the right's *alter ego*; of yet another slow-motion kamikaze act, like Scargill's; of declining and divided Labour, saddled with impossible municipal problems; and of populist left policies (in a dying landscape) whose macho-'socialism' is merely a crude – even criminalized – workerism shored up by welfare, and more plebeian than proletarian.

The price being exacted by all the muscle and bluster is heavy; the local trade unions, the black community, the local Labour Party are being torn asunder. As soon as we begin talking, John Hamilton, Labour's Militant-surrounded, and Quaker, city council leader – a genial but exhausted Pickwickian figure, paunched in a grey pullover under creased pinstripe – unceremoniously calls Militant 'an underground organization', with 'tentacles' to boot; and complains, looking over his shoulder at the Militant-dominated District Labour Party whose decisions dictate those of the city council, that 'I'm a leader, but I don't have power'. Promptly backtracking, he then declares that 'I might deplore certain things, but I can't disentangle myself from the broad policy, because I'm with it'; and (more strongly) that 'I have absolute sympathy for what we are doing.' What are you doing? 'We're doing our best to kick the Tories in the teeth,' he replies, at the same time claiming that he gets letters 'from all over the country, saying, "Good on you, we're glad someone is standing up to them." ' And temporarily regaining his uncomfortable perch as Liverpool's piggie-in-the-middle, he adds that 'there's a strong groundswell of support for socialism in this city, from all classes'.

But (mere moments later) he declares, under his breath and his short-lived confidence suddenly flagging, that 'the Government would like to keep Militant here as long as they can'. Why? 'Because Militant has become a dirty word, a word to

whip people with.' Do you think then, I ask him, that
Labour's national prospects will be damaged by the Liverpool
shemozzle? 'I'm not in any doubt of it,' he answered wearily,
one of the old school of municipal Labour and stuck –
leaden-footed – deep in his contradictions.

It was after 6 p.m., the town hall silent, Hamilton's deputy
– the wire-haired political fox-terrier, Derek Hatton – off the
premises (and avoiding interview), his next-door room deserted. 'Militant', Hamilton suddenly says as I am writing, 'are
trying to box me off from the media.' How? 'If you go through
to the Unit' – the euphemism for Militant's 'inner circle of
hard-left media handlers' (*Liverpool Echo*), installed along the
corridor – 'they'll tell you I'm out, when I'm in.' What are you
saying, exactly? 'They push me in the background. The press
is not helping me, not helping the situation. The press ought
to be recognizing me as leader. Instead, it's given Militant an
enormous public image. It would have cost them millions.'

(The Unit's job, the town hall Militants tell you – 'we've got
nothing to hide' – is to be 'responsive to the political programmes of the council', as well as to 'deal quickly with allegations
about expensive cars and chauffeurs'. But 'some of the journalists that we won't speak to are only after Derek Hatton's dirty
bedsheets from Bournemouth, just filth'. What they call the
'traditional PR game' – described to me as ' "Eating Out In
Liverpool", Beatles' maps, planting Christmas trees and kis-
sing babies' – has been 'reallocated downwards'. The heavy
stuff is in the hands of Andrew ('Andy') Pink, 'city propaganda supremo', according to the *Liverpool Echo*. A pale, close-
cut young chap, in Militant's rimless specs and an expensive
light blue suede jacket, he has an uneasily cross-class, or
quasi-proletarian, manner. The son of a prominent local Tory
major, and himself 'a Tory, pre-Grunwick', Pink was to say to
me later that Hamilton ('a bit hostile to Militant') was
'nobody's fool', but that 'the media demands Derek'. Why?
'Because he's more interesting,' he had replied, with a dead-
pan expression.)

There is a further pause as I write, Hamilton, a former

science-teacher at a comprehensive in Kirkby, looking at me. 'How much', he continues, 'is Militant, how much is gangster-ism?' What do you mean? 'All the council security men are Militant. Militants in the trade unions vet all the appoint-ments. You can't get a job in the town hall unless you're a Militant. We've got the Mafia in here,' he goes on wanly, 'a Chicago, Mayor Daley-type situation. It's the first time it's come into England.' (He then referred to Eric Heffer as a 'close friend'. Does he agree with what you're saying? 'Yes, he does.' Why doesn't he say it? 'He couldn't.') As for the thirty-seven-year-old Hatton himself, an Everton fan with a blank, shining face – who says he 'hates being scruffy' and has a habit of shutting his eyes when talking people down in discussion – 'his life-style', says Hamilton, 'is not that of a socialist, with those flashy cars and that expensive style of living'. What is he up to then? 'He's just using the Labour Party as a springboard into national prominence. He's actually said [where?] that if he wasn't Labour, he'd be Tory.'

As it happens, it was the 'death-agonies' of international capitalism which were Trotsky's main subject, not these provincial knackers' yards of labour. 'This place is even bugged,' says Hamilton, helplessly (or hopelessly) genial. The leader of the Liverpool city council then got up from his desk, portly, his jacket lapels food-stained, and opened the door dividing his office from Hatton's. On Hatton's desk ('here, look at this') was an innocent-looking TV console, its blue screen showing the corridor outside and a passing janitor – or, perhaps, a member of the 'Static Security Force', which the local rags allege to be Hatton's private army, one of whose supervisors has a 1981 conviction for malicious wounding. ('There are some right lumpen elements in the Static,' I was told later by a local trade union official, who did not want to be named.) Hamilton then bent over the screen in all his civic majesty, and turned up the sound. You could hear every footfall, or every whisper.

'You are in a schizophrenic position,' he said, returning to his office, and sitting down heavily. 'I have thought of resigning. But the issue is not just Militant, or getting hold of money. The issue is winning back local autonomy and demo-cratic powers from a domineering government in Whitehall. That's why I am standing and fighting my corner, instead of blaming Militant for their tactics,' he adds, meeting himself coming backwards again, but still smiling. 'And there are those who see me as a white hope.' Why? 'Because I can get on with everybody, including those I don't agree with. I have to stand shoulder-to-shoulder with all shades. If I go, you can imagine what would happen.' What would happen? I ask him. 'Everything disappears,' he replied, his plump hands clasped before him at the polished town hall table.

'He hasn't got the guts of a louse,' says thickset Tony McGann, the militant anti-Militant vice-chairman of the Catholic Vauxhall Ward Labour Party, speaking of Hamilton. 'The man's petrified of them, that's God's truth.' He recalls a recent private – or secret – meeting with the council leader. 'I was telling him, "Stand up to them Militants, John", but his mouth was quivering, he was that terrified of being seen with us from Vauxhall. He kept looking round like this,' says McGann, neck-folds turning, blarney embroidering the re-cord. 'When he left, he pulled his hat down, and his coat collar up, he was that scared, he was shaking. I felt really sorry for him, as a man,' McGann adds tenderly, his pugnacious phiz an emblem of God-fearing commiseration.

The beefed-up ward party now has 200 members, 90 per cent of them unemployed and 103 of them drummed in, in September 1983, to drive out the ward's then controlling Militant caucus. 'You're dealing with an organization of thugs,' McGann claims – pawing the ground as the red flag flutters before him – who not only 'bus children to certain schools for political education', but have 'threatened Breck Road market traders', occupying a site wanted by the council, 'with sawn-off shotguns'. McGann ('we were more cuter than them'), fists at rest in his lap, looks as if he can take care of himself in this kind of paranoid ding-dong. 'We've got more socialism in our little fingers', he added, 'than Militants have got in their whole bodies.'

Wearing dark-tinted specs, his thick wrist in a silver bracelet, McGann doubles up in the district as the 'dynamo' of the Eldonian Community Association, a neighbourhood housing co-operative. Set up to redeem an area 'smashed up when they built the Mersey Tunnel' – which 'took away people's roots' and 'broke their hearts' – the co-operative itself 'hit a brick wall' as soon as Labour, and Militant, came back to local power in 1983. 'The first thing they done', he says bitterly, 'was to freeze the lot. Whoever thought Labour would do a thing like that to our people? The co-op was like a dream to them.' To hear him talk, jowls a-quiver ('people have the right to a say about the way they're living'), the 'Corpy' (Corporation) was without mercy; wanting to 'centralize everything' in the interest of the Direct Works department, and putting town hall-directed council house building, not co-operatives, on top of their housing agenda. Co-operatives are in any case seen by Militant as a legacy of the 'Liberal-Tory regime' which ran the city from 1974 to 1983; the 'heart of socialism' to McGann – for which belief he claims he is greeted by Militant 'catcalls, jeering and shouting' at meetings – is no more than 'co-operative privatization' to the city's left hardliners.

Here in Vauxhall ('there's no one suffering more than us') bitterness and bleakness – of huge local unemployment, housing ruin, closed-down factory sites and internecine political struggle within the ranks of Labour – are heaped upon each other; 'the real Labour feelings', Sir Trevor Jones, the Liberal leader, called them later. In the community office, the angry or desperate talk, in the remains of Irish brogue, is variously of 'professional people coming here to write their books on inner city problems' – 'we'd like to march the lot of them down to the Liverpool canal and throw them in' – or 'using this area as just a stepping stone to the Home Office'; and of their own success ('we've got some strong lads of our own') in 'knocking Militant pig-sick' by packing the ward party with members of the housing co-operative, after it had been 'kicked into touch' by the 'town hall centralizers'. According to McGann, seething, the rival mob have even 'posted their minders up from London' to local ward meetings; 'with noses like this' – violently flattening his own nose with two pudgy fingers – and 'threatening to burn people'. (Come back Sidney Webb, all is forgiven.) 'If Militant want your opinion, they'll give it to you,' McGann added sourly, overstewed in his own juices. 'But nobody's backing off round here. For every Militant they put in to Vauxhall, we'll put another ten of our lads in,' he says, as if itching for a punch-up.

John Livingston, the ward chairman (or precinct boss) then appeared in the Eldonian office. Calling himself a 'lifelong Christian [i.e. Catholic] socialist' – and describing Militant as a 'repulsive left-wing fascist organization' of 'cold-blooded gangsters' – he turns out to be a jabbing, fifty-plus lightweight in this multi-ring Tammany circus. He describes Vauxhall as a 'closely-knit community which has got its identity from our Irish forebears'; himself joined the Labour Party 'only three or four years ago'; and has told local party objectors to his ban on Militant to 'visit a taxidermist'. With green CND and NUPE badges in his lapel, he is spry and sharp in jeans, highly polished black shoes and a neat blue padded anorak; takes ginseng and health food; and has been a university technician, worked on building sites, and serviced electronic equipment, until being swallowed up in the tide of Liverpool unemployment.

Twiddling his car keys, dapper and greying, Livingston declares that the Labour Party 'accords with my Christian background'; and, with a plastic bag of Marks and Spencer shopping on the chair beside him, says that 'freedom of choice is what democratic socialism is all about'. He is in regular correspondence on the subject of Militant with Neil Kinnock. To Livingston, Trotskyism and Toryism are 'at opposite poles of the same evil', and 'against the interests of ordinary people', while Militant's description of this Vauxhall Labour outfit as a 'right-wing Catholic Mafia' he dismisses as 'blasphemy'.

'We've been the most reasonable of people,' he claims, but talks with thin-lipped gusto of the town hall's 'crimes', 'lies' and 'evil'. 'I've told Kinnock', he continues – 'if he doesn't act, he's as bad as they are,' McGann interrupted – 'that with all the suffering of our country under the reign of Thatcher, the only thing that will stop Labour is what Militant is doing. And if the most warrior-like union, such as the NUM, couldn't defeat that stone-hearted woman, how is a bunch of council workers in Liverpool going to do it?' No one answers, the silence an inner one. Beyond the window of the community office is a blasted terrain of abandoned workplaces – the Tate and Lyle refinery among them – and forlorn Victorian church-granite. Outside, the spirit and the eye are repelled together; inside, Trotskyism, to them, is 'tyranny', while the Russians, according to Livingston, citing Bishop Fulton Sheen and gathering up his shopping, 'when they outgrow their communist quirk, will one day be in the forefront of a world-wide Christian renewal'.

It seems to be one damned obsession after another: a politics of infiltration, investigation ('witch hunts') and counter-investigation; of reselection, deselection and disqualification; of plain fisticuffs and complex faction struggles, even enlivened – according to Ian Williams, guru of the anti-Militant Liverpool Labour Left, itself set up under the auspices of *Tribune* – by threats of a spot of fraternal leg-breaking. Jovial, ginger-bearded and in his late thirties, Williams ('we want to eliminate the category of thought-crimes') presides over his own left salon in the book-lined front room of his Victorian terrace, the upper panes of the leaded bay-windows fruit-decorated. An ex-bus conductor, ex-glass worker, ex-steel worker, ex-adult student, and now a BR guard on long-term sick leave, he speaks of Militant as a 'marginal group of pariahs' – even, a 'closed, Panglossian circle' – 'offering to do untold damage to themselves, and [laughing uproariously] expecting a Tory government to come in and help them out of it'. 'He spends most of his time writing in journals like the *New Statesman*,' said Tony Mulhearn later, through the side of his mouth. 'It seems to be his main aim in life; I don't know what his game is.'

To Williams, amid his spider-plants and first editions – and himself a Birchite Maoist in the 1970s – Militancy, Liverpool-style, is the 'psychopathology of politics' and 'a matter of delusion'. (In turn, *they* speak of *his* group as 'just a bunch of weak characters, pissed-off people'.) 'Those who tell the truth here', he continues, 'are immediately denounced as traitors. And then, when reality and theory turn out not to match, or when the distance between them grows wider and wider, they've always got to be looking for somebody else to blame for it.' Nevertheless, he admits both that 'Militant has had the initiative on every front', and that there is a 'genuine resonance at the bedrock level of Liverpool chauvinism' for what he calls 'simplistic political programmes', and 'pure headbanging'. But aren't Militant 'defending working-class interests', like they say? 'For them, the working class is a political, not social definition.' What do you mean? 'I mean you can live in one room in Liverpool 8, but as soon as you disagree with them, you'll become an instant petit-bourgeois.' Behind him the painted fruit, in their leaded panes, are a blushing pink, or roseate, and wreathed in honey-yellow garlands. 'One of my hobbies has always been Byzantine history. It has stood me in good stead,' says Williams, laughing again.

But the naked eye will do for a start, if you want to make sense of the stony heart of the problem. It's in all this boarded-up Gothic; in the bared roof-timbers and unshifted garbage; in the blank brick-walls of Liverpool warehouses, Alsatian-guarded, the padlocked iron rusting. This is a city slowly being gutted, where the council is the largest employer (31,000), and Littlewood's (14,000) is the second; where new corporation greensward has been laid in a landscaped desert: of housing estates set down in a new form of 'regenerated' dereliction, where beaten-up cars roar down the dual carriageways with no chance of take-off, the city's vistas turned to ribbon concrete. Friday mid-afternoons, a dreary mile from the city centre, are as depopulated as a southern Sunday.

In the sales manager's oily-carpeted cabin at Martindale and Carlyle's garage ('Your Nissan Dealer: Most Reliably Yours'), the four-man inner circle of Liverpool Against Militant has its heads down for a planning meeting. This is some kind of anti-collective crusade; 'Your City Needs You! Save Liverpool!' implore their leaflets. Here, among the Japanese Cherries, Sunnys, and Stanzas are club-owner John Jones ('We've made it on our own in life, we're a group of individuals, not marchers'), who is an ex-coal-merchant and former night-club bouncer at Flintlock's in Seal Street; forty-three-year-old garage managing director Jeff Tinnion, round-shouldered in a light blue check jacket, brown pipe-burn marks above his breast-pocket; in large green specs, Jackie Samuels – 'he started the whole thing,' says Jones – the Atherton Road kitchen outfitter, wearing a damask shirt and woman's pink cardigan, his blonded hair cut in a fetching tousle; and the reticent Mike Byrne (with a missing thumb and damaged finger-tips), former compère at Russell's night club in Parr Street and 'promotions manager' of a local free-sheet, who also runs a keep-fit joint called Bodyshape.

'Definitely Poujadist,' declared Ian Williams, of the lot of them; according to Labour councillor Mike Black, their politics are those 'of the Orange Lodge and the British Movement'. To Tony Mulhearn, the garage mob are 'enraged petits-bourgeois'; to Sir Trevor Jones, 'a very good cross-section of loyal Liverpudlians, first and foremost'. 'Ordinary business people who want a Labour government, because they're going bankrupt under the Tories,' was John Livingston's description of them, but he denied every claim that he had attended and spoken at their meetings; 'I know one or two of them', was all that he was admitting.

Garage-boss Tinnion ('I'm a Tory, nationally'), working-class, from Knotty Ash and 'brought up in a council house', is an ex-police cadet, son of a 'well-known Liverpool bobby', and a serving member of a local DHSS appeals tribunal, which adjudicates on dole entitlement, child benefit and sickness benefit cases. His dad, he says with quiet pride, 'got the BEM in 1961 for disarming a nigger'; he himself was nominated *Auto Advertiser*'s 'Dealer of the Week' in August 1984, and 'runs' a Nissan Sylvia Turbo. As for John Jones ('I'm a socialist, I'd never vote Thatcher'), who has his hair in rats' tails and Michael Crick's book on Militant among his papers, he has 'nothing against Trotskyist ideas, as such'. (It's 'Militant's corruption' he objects to.) 'In a democracy', the club owner continues, 'they're entitled to stand up for their politics, provided they do it under their own banner.' But the trouble is that Liverpool is 'very vulnerable'. To what? 'With the docks diminishing,' he replies, 'we're ripe for exploitation by extremists.' 'We're easygoing people,' chips in Tinnion. 'And when you get an extreme left like them, you'll end up with an extreme right to fight them,' Jones added. There is a moment of anxious assent in the cabin; what they call 'boss politics' is getting to them. The rows of burnished Nissan Bluebirds stand in wait for their HP buyers.

'We've got to educate the people', declares Tinnion, pipe in hand and with his monthly sales-charts pinned to the softboard wall beside him, 'that Militant are going for revolution.' 'We've only got one aim,' adds Byrne ('I'm a Tory-Liberal') from the depths of the cabin sofa, 'and that's to get Militant out of this city.' Tinnion, his hair styled and cut like a close-fitting helmet, taps his pipe out into the metal ashtray. 'We might come across as right-wing Tories,' says Jones (the Club), 'but Vauxhall Ward are completely behind us. They get called scabs and Tory-lovers, but they don't recognize Militant, what they recognize is the Labour Party. No one's letting a bunch of law-breakers run our city,' the ex-bouncer added. With their own campaign being 'pushed on by the public', they are currently 'marketing a disc' of their Pier Head rally speeches and songs – it includes, for £1.50, 'There Is A Green Hill Far Away' and John Lennon's 'Imagine' – as well as lapel stickers with the legend 'I Ain't Afraid Of No Trots', and a four-page hand-out called *Trotbuster*. 'With their hair cut short, these Trots are trying to create a nice, clean-cut image, like the Mormons,' continues Jones, twenty years spent on the old coal wagons and doing most of the gang's talking. 'They have this religious zeal, they want to control everything. If they fail, they've got a scorched earth policy. They'll destruct the lot. They're an élitist, left-wing group who've got everybody by the balls in this city. They're not true Labour, sharing things out, they're more interested in business, like that capitalist Hatton. We want people to see Militant as an evil, corrupt power,' he adds, his shoes dusty and the mood in the cabin hardening, 'as a dirty name, like "Nazis".' At this point, the silent Samuels had to 'dash'; getting up and drawing his coat around him, in a kind of self-hugging. 'A really lovely fella,' the others said of him when he'd gone; as the door opened, you could see the Japanese car bonnets ranged in multicoloured serried ranks, the showroom walls hung with Christmas bunting.

A silence then fell upon the car seller's tat and the stream-lined brochures. And Kinnock? 'He says he's going to kick the American bases out of the UK,' John Jones answered for the others, 'but he can't even kick the bloody Trots out of this city. But if Militant get hold of the country, it will be like Nazi Germany in the 1930s.' When I left, the cabin meeting was still in session, the apocalypse its agenda.

'It's been vitriolic,' said Liberal leader Sir Trevor Jones in his warehouse office in Lydia Ann Street, preoccupied with bond notes and tons of bananas, ships' sailing times and cargoes of refrigerated mutton. 'But we can dish it out, too. You've got to, or you wouldn't survive here. It's the roughest and toughest forum in the country'; even kindly old John Hamilton, mixing it himself, called him a 'lifelong Tory trader'. Moreover, it is a forum convulsed by 'a struggle between liberty and totalitarianism', in which every civic virtue – to judge by what Sir Trevor is saying – is in danger of coming a cropper. 'What you are witnessing here', he declares, 'is a revolution.' A revolution? 'A mini-revolution.' But then he himself attended Liverpool Against Militant's founding meeting.

A ship's rigger by trade, ex-T & G, who 'walked up and

down the docks for fourteen years', the Liberal leader fishes in a quality tomato box for the old annual reports of the Liverpool housing directorate, in order to refute Labour denunciations of the Liberals' housing record. 'A lot of the stuff you see on site is what we put in,' he says, in blue check shirt, pullover and hand-tailored flannels; 'if they say the houses are not there, then they must be hanging on sky-hooks'. Yet the period of Liberal rule was one of relatively low-level town hall spending – 'a toytown council', Tony McGann called it, 'when 5,000 jobs were lost', according to Hatton – but which was, subsequently, to provide the bench-mark for the city's Whitehall-fixed spending targets. Never-theless, Sir Trevor claims that in 1983 the Liberals handed over to the incoming Labour administration 'ample' credit balances of £38·1 million, 'together with what I call the money in our back-pockets'; complains that 'all rational discussion has since been swept away in Liverpool'; and accuses the city's non-Militant Labour MPs, such as Heffer, of 'letting Militant completely mesmerize them. When you switch them [Mili-tant] on, they all say the same things. Put a gag on Tony Mulhearn, and the next one will simply take over.'

At a desk cluttered with steamship company invoices, the former rigger, smoking a Hamlet, describes how he loads his own wagons at the market. 'I buy all the fruit and veg at four every morning, but Hatton goes about in a chauffeur-driven car with two minders. And *he* talks about the working class,' he adds, laughing, an eczematous rash on his forehead. (Sir Trevor then claimed that Lord (Bill) Sefton, a previous Liverpool Labour boss, 'always says I should have been Labour. But I'm a libertarian.') 'Militant would have given anyone the town hall clock to get power. From the word "go" they were in trouble, hooked on their own lies, with policies of no rate increases, inflation, and, on top of it, making a sacred cow of their housing programme.' They were not only 'ruth-less, authoritarian die-hards' who 'drove everything through the council committees', continues Sir Trevor ('I want to devolve power, give people control over their own lives'), but incompetent into the bargain, their political campaigns a 'confidence trick', and 'as bogus as a two-pound note'. They even 'brainwashed their troops into believing that they would have to man the barricades', he adds, laughing like a drain. 'Where they were efficient', he says, his eyes crow's-footed, a long uncut nail on his little finger, 'was the way they carried out the whole political operation. They infiltrated the union branches first, then the ward parties. The last thing was to take over the elected positions, when' – holding his hands up, palms flat towards me – 'the whole thing was in place for them.'

He is using the past tense. Indeed, if the High Court were now to disqualify the forty-eight Labour city councillors (some of them on the dole) who voted the 9 per cent illegal rate in June 1985 – 'illegal', under the 1982 Act, because too low to cover planned council spending – a rump of thirty Liberals would take over 'to sort out the mess' until there were new municipal elections. 'And when that happens,' declared Liverpool's knight-errant in his waterfront warehouse, 'I'm going to have to hold our people back, and say, "No, you're not going to pay off old scores, there'll be no reprisals." ' That is, Liberal chivalries will be restored, and *omertà* itself outlawed, as the city carries on down the Swanee. But why, I ask him, are you using the past tense about Labour? 'I don't want to crow about what Militant have done to the Labour Party,' he replied, crowing, 'but politically, they're all walking corpses. They're dead. When they're going to lie down is the only question.'

Not for Tony Mulhearn, NGA compositor and Militant president of the District Labour Party, it isn't. Accused locally of being 'organ grinder to Hatton's monkey', and coming across as the lantern-jawed *éminence grise* of a sect of emotionally full-time political Moonies, he shows up at his well-appointed open-plan semi in a natty dove-grey tracksuit. 'He's got five hairdressing establishments,' John Livingston had said, ducking in close and rabbit-punching, 'he's doing very well under Thatcher.' Certainly the Militants are stern working-class purists when it comes to the bourgeois or, worse, the petit-bourgeois. But bearded in his own suburban lair, or class no man's land, in Broadgreen – where Hatton also lives – you'll find that it is all tapestry-upholstered lounge-suites, expensive electronics and rubber plants, upwardly aspiring.

For the last few months challenging the Labour MP Robert Kilroy-Silk (a 'potential defector like Reg Prentice') for the parliamentary nomination in Knowsley, Mulhearn has Trotsky's *Third International after Lenin*, Howard Fast's *Spartacus*, Shirley Conran's *Lace 2* and a biography of Frank Sinatra on his bookshelves; and scattered on his study's cord-carpeted floor, beneath the stereo-player, are 'Relax with Richard Clayderman', Jennifer Rush's 'The Power of Love' and Wham!'s 'Last Christmas'. The Liverpool Labour Party, over which he presides, he calls 'an institution which has seen charlatans come and go, people who have got no history in the Liverpool movement, who don't understand the roots of the Labour tradition'; unlike those he impassively calls the 'genuine, indigenous comrades'. ('If you go up to the panel that chooses Labour candidates for the council,' said Tony McGann, 'it's the likes of him who's doing the interviewing.') Beyond the pale of political authenticity stands the new Liverpool Labour Left caucus; 'we've asked them to debate with us, but with no alternative policy they'd have been blasted out of the ground', as Mulhearn puts it, a ribboned guitar hanging on the wall before him. 'But we won't be demanding expulsions or proscriptions,' he asserts chuckling briefly, or very briefly. This entryist poacher has turned gamekeeper of the inner party. 'I'm Liverpool Labour Left myself, I might even join them,' he added, mordant as a stone, Petula Clark on the carpet beside his chair-leg.

Smooth – 'it's only people not confident of their positions who resort to vilification of their opponents' – he is clean-shaven and greying; a 'quiet figure', the ship's chandler had surprisingly called him. In a sweat-shirt with green border ('he probably works out on a punchbag,' said Tony McGann), he asserts, comfortable in the chaos, that 'we'll get a financial package together to see us through to April', and into what he calls the 'regrouping of our forces' and the 'next stage of the struggle'. What struggle? There is a head-high embankment of Avis 1600 video equipment in the room's corner. 'A major challenge to the government's policy of undermining local democracy,' Mulhearn answers. 'And if what they did to the miners is a guide,' he adds, 'we can guess what they'll be trying to do to us for it.' Our conversation was then interrupted by a long phone-call from 'Eddie', another 'reader of the *Militant* newspaper'. Throughout the call, Mulhearn was monosyllabic, or silent – except once to ask, 'How many members have you got?' Resuming, Mulhearn says of council leader John Hamilton that 'there is tremendous respect and affection for him in the movement. I've got a lot of respect for him myself,' he declares, further calling him the 'cream of respectability'. Do you mean he's middle-class? 'He's not what you'd describe as a horny-handed son of toil, is he?' Mulhearn answers, his eyes lighting up for a moment; 'I suppose he moves in those kinds of circles,' he added blankly. 'But you've got to give it to him. He understands what the game is, he by no means lacks perception. On the question of policy, he's solid. And there's not a nasty bone in his body'; he's just nervous about Hatton's closed-circuit television.

Mulhearn's spleen is reserved for the press ('conspiracies, Militant this, Militant that, campaigning against us at a far more higher crescendo'); for the 'Vauxhall crowd' ('they don't have a political base. They're being investigated by the regional party for unconstitutional action'); and for the 'reckless' Neil Kinnock ('what determines his overall strategy are the leader-writers of the serious Fleet Street papers'). Sitting still in his chair, and almost without moving a muscle, Mulhearn denounces the Labour leader for 'hitting at Liverpool'; says that 'the miners detest him, except in Nottingham' and that he's done 'enormous damage to his own position'. In what way? 'You wouldn't have a Labour movement at all without the kind of people he's been attacking. The signifi-

cance of what the man stands for has not been lost,' he adds
darkly. What are you threatening? 'We have the job of trying
to influence him,' he replies, side-stepping, 'as long as he
remains leader.' Influence him to do what? 'To get him back
on the road of Clause Four, defending the democratic gains of
the labour movement, rebuilding the mass party.' And hard as
nails – dug in, not bunkered – he declares that 'they won't shift
Militant out tomorrow'. 'It's up in the air with a shower of
sparks and down to earth again, like a November the Fifth
rocket,' said Eddie Bannon; 'they'll disappear like snow off the
roofs,' said Sir Trevor. At parting, Mulhearn – who shows no
sign of being on the ropes, or even off-balance – has a friendly
handshake; with the same neatly cut short hair as all the
others.

But then working-class (or ex-working-class) scousers –
streetwise fixers and fighters, Mulhearn and Hatton, Trevor
Jones and Eric Heffer, Livingston, McGann, and John Jones,
all Liverpool-loyal and with a strange relish for trouble – have
more in common than divides them, as the city (strapped for
cash, 'being skinned alive', or an 'infected wound', according
to judgment) slugs it out with Whitehall. 'They always knew
they were going to go bust, they always knew they faced
disqualification, they always knew they would split the labour
movement,' complained Geoff Burgess, the bitterly anti-
Militant chairman of the City branch of NALGO. 'It's a great
struggle of the people of Liverpool, as simple as that,'
exploded the owlish Heffer – 'he's gone completely dingo,'
said Ian Williams – shouting like Desperate Dan (amid the
Commons' teacup clatter) that his alleged 'fear of Militant' was
a 'load of old cobblers' and a 'bloody lie'. The walrus and
carpenter in one, Heffer seems to inhabit his own private
shambles. 'I was there', he noisily declares, heads turning, and
stirring his tea as if with a trowel, 'in the days when the
Braddocks organized, and when the Seftons organized against
the Braddocks', for all the world like the Guelphs and the
Ghibellines, or the Mods and Rockers. 'They just don't know
me, mate!' (they do). 'It's always gone on!' (what has?); and,

supping loudly, 'I've never been a Militant!' he shouts (who the hell said he had been?). 'I've never been in groups, I haven't got the bloody time for it, I'm opposed to what they are saying!' I see. 'But I'm against witch hunts, I'm against expulsions!' He looks at me, truculent and blinking like a koala, wet lower lip hanging; 'I don't make deals with anybody,' he raucously added (though no one had suggested that either), still in disarray at the original insult.

'For the first time in their lives', he insists, 'the working class of Liverpool feels confident. They're prepared to fight. If they go down,' he says, 'the effect will be disastrous for the whole movement, bloody disastrous! But the whole business of Militant is being exaggerated,' he suddenly declares, as if losing his stuffing, 'they're not real problems at all.' Oh? 'The trouble is being caused by a small group of people.' Which group of people? 'A small group of people,' he says testily, exasperated, 'who don't like Militant. Maybe I'm naive,' he adds, quieter at last, and pushing away his teacup in its slopped saucer, 'but the media is reading far too much into it. And let me tell you this,' he says, pointing his finger at me, 'Liverpool people don't like anyone coming up and telling them what they should be doing. They don't now, they never did, and they never will.' 'It's different if a scouser does it,' said Eddie Bannon.

Indeed, when defiant ranks close against the outsider, even that self-consuming proletarian envy which identifies those who have 'got on' – like Hatton – as 'snappy dressers' or 'Volvo owners' can turn, despite the anger at Militant policy, to admiration for the 'tireless' or 'dedicated' Liverpudlian defender – like Hatton – struggling in the penalty area, and always ready to put the boot in. And then, what is 'autocratic centralism' (or 'gangsterism') to some, becomes a big, fast town hall forward-line to others, shooting first and asking questions after. 'The forty-eight would do it again tomorrow,' they tell you proudly; *cui bono?* is another matter. Doing the Tories' work for them Militant may be, and beyond the Tories' wildest expectations; or digging their own political graves, sleeves rolled up and eyes shining. But, up here, 'people don't believe you can be fighting unless you're bleed- ing', as Ian Williams put it. 'Fighting to give people hope,' 'Andy' Pink, the ex-Tory media handler, called it, his accent turning more scouse with each sentence. ('And if you haven't got hope,' he added, specs catching the light, 'what have you got?') Even 'going down with dignity' – and going down this city is, like Byzantium in the time of Severus – has its own, Liverpudlian value.

Afterword

In Hyde, they stopped publishing the town's employment statistics, David Livingstone retired, his Newton patient died of her cancer, and his former practice was computerizing its medical records.

In Wolverhampton, John Clifford's 'People's Centre' failed to get off the ground, unemployment rose to 20·2 per cent, Ian Philips continued in the Careers Office, Christine Atherton joined the Socialist Workers' Party and Jack Jones became a student.

In Sheffield, tiring of the battle with Whitehall, David Blunkett – promoted to the NEC of the Labour Party – was nominated to the 'safe' parliamentary seat of Brightside, Roy Thwaites toyed with, and under pressure dropped, a patronage job winding up his own South Yorkshire county council, and bus fares rose 250 per cent after its abolition.

In Birmingham, Hyacinth Wilson got into trouble with the local authority for what she had told me, Colvin Marshall and Joe Lee remained jobless, Uncle Sam's travel agency was looted in the Handsworth riots, and the black exodus continued, even if some of the interviewees (such as Hubert Tulloch) were 'still plodding along' in the city.

In Fleet, Neil and Suzanne Jones were facing 'harder times' as farmers, Eric Green was 'encouraged by the SDP's progress', Richard Barlow – now cleaning up in Singapore – was finding the entrepreneurial going rougher, Tony Hancock was more opposed than ever to the politics of Mrs Thatcher, and Nick Green had become a 'territory salesman' for Kelloggs.

In Bradford, Mike Whittaker was transferred to the Home

Office, Mohammed Ajeeb became Lord Mayor (with an Imam as his civic chaplain), Ray Honeyford was pursued into enforced retirement, and two members of the anti-Honeyford parents' committee were reported to have visited Colonel Gaddafi.

In Doncaster, the critics of Arthur Scargill felt themselves vindicated by the miners' failure, George Moores ran into local difficulties for his remarks to me about Gerald Kaufman and Leon Brittan, while Askern police station was greeted on Guy Fawkes night, 1985, seven months after the miners' strike was over, with a hail of stones and milk bottles.

In Meirionnydd, Trawsfynydd nuclear power station sprang a leak, bilingualism remained a battlefield, Dafydd Elis Thomas marched through Blaenau in support of striking quarrymen – with Owen Edwards collecting funds, but criticized in the town as 'lukewarm' – and Plaid Cymru's 'Gramscian' left remained in the ascendant in the party.

In Liverpool, Derek Hatton and Tony Mulhearn were expelled from the Labour Party, Vauxhall's John Livingston was placed on Labour's panel of prospective municipal candidates, and Labour councillors – John Hamilton included – brought appeals, at a cost of hundreds of thousands of pounds, against their High Court disqualifications from office.